Break the
Co-Sleeping
Habit

Break the Co-Sleeping Habit

How to Set Bedtime Boundaries—
and Raise a Secure, Happy,
Well-Adjusted Child

VALERIE LEVINE, PH.D.

Aadamsmedia
Avon, Massachusetts

Published by
Adams Media, a division of F+W Media, Inc.
57 Littlefield Street, Avon, MA 02322. U.S.A.
www.adamsmedia.com

ISBN-13: 978-1-59869-901-2
ISBN-10: 1-59869-901-6

Printed in the United States of America.

J I H G F E D C B A

Library of Congress Cataloging-in-Publication Data
is available from the publisher.

This publication is designed to provide accurate and authoritative information with
regard to the subject matter covered. It is sold with the understanding that the publisher
is not engaged in rendering legal, accounting, or other professional advice. If legal advice
or other expert assistance is required, the services of a competent professional person
should be sought.
—From a *Declaration of Principles* jointly adopted by a Committee of the
American Bar Association and a Committee of Publishers and Associations

Many of the designations used by manufacturers and sellers to distinguish their product
are claimed as trademarks. Where those designations appear in this book and Adams
Media was aware of a trademark claim, the designations have been printed with initial
capital letters.

This book is available at quantity discounts for bulk purchases.
For information, please call 1-800-289-0963.

Acknowledgments

I would like to express appreciation to:

My friend, Liz Caran, LCSW, for sharing her insights into family dynamics and for her support of this project;

My colleagues, Dr. Jim Horwitz and Dr. Paul Iacono, for their time and for their openness to combining medical with psychological approaches;

My agent, Gina Panettieri, whose enthusiasm and insight were instrumental in providing me the opportunity to communicate with parents beyond the walls of the therapy office;

My stepdaughter, Jessica, for our special relationship; and

My husband, Andrew, for his belief in me always.

Contents

1 INTRODUCTION

PART I: STAYING ATTACHED WITHOUT CO-SLEEPING

11 CHAPTER 1 ■ Attachment During Infancy and Beyond

31 CHAPTER 2 ■ Why Are You Co-Sleeping?

41 CHAPTER 3 ■ Further Benefits of Independent Sleep

PART II: HOW TO BREAK THE CO-SLEEPING HABIT

65 CHAPTER 4 ■ How to Become a Calm, Assertive Leader in Your Home

73 CHAPTER 5 ■ How to Challenge Your Inner Barriers

97 CHAPTER 6 ■ How to Set Limits with Your Toddler and Preschooler

117 CHAPTER 7 ■ How to Teach Your Elementary School Child to Sleep Without You

145 CHAPTER 8 ■ How to Intervene with Preteens and Teens

161 CHAPTER 9 ■ How to Deal with Special Situations

PART III: A CLOSER LOOK AT FAMILIES IN THE CO-SLEEPING HABIT

171   CHAPTER 10 ▪ Tucking In That Never Ends

179   CHAPTER 11 ▪ The Middle-of-the-Night Wake-Up Call

185   CHAPTER 12 ▪ Your Child Starts Off in Your Bed and Never Leaves

191   CHAPTER 13 ▪ Sneaking into Your Bed "Unnoticed"

197   CHAPTER 14 ▪ The Divorced or Single Parent

205   CHAPTER 15 ▪ The Ultimate Co-Sleep Imbalance

211   CONCLUSION

221   INDEX

229   ABOUT THE AUTHOR

INTRODUCTION

I f you are co-sleeping with a child between the ages of two
and eighteen years old, but you don't really want to, you
are not alone. Maybe you wanted to co-sleep and you have
changed your mind—but your child hasn't. Maybe you started
co-sleeping after infancy to comfort your child, and now it's a
habit that has gotten out of control. Do you feel exhausted from
bedtime power struggles, so you just give in? I wrote this book so
that you can teach your children how to sleep without you and
feel good about it.

In some families, co-sleeping, or sleep sharing, works. In those
families, the parents are willing participants, the co-sleeping
was intentional, and there was a planned or natural transition to
independent sleep.

However, in many families co-sleeping is a habit that parents
don't know how to break. In these families, one or both parents
are reluctant participants. The parents are controlled by their
children's unreasonable behavior or by their own insecurities
about being decision-makers.

When co-sleeping is a habit, the nighttime scene may go
something like this. One or both parents guide the children
through a bedtime routine. They tuck the children in. Then, at
some point during the tucking in process, one or more of the
children wants something—a drink of water, another trip to the

bathroom, another story, or something else. One of the parents provides the thing—whatever it is—but either it was provided imperfectly ("This water is yucky!"), or there is another request, and then another. The parent provides each thing, tries really hard to do it perfectly, and when at a point of saturation, tells the child to go to sleep. The child starts to whine or cry. If there are other children, they might chime in—or not, if you're lucky. The parent, and maybe by now the other parent, tries to reason with the children. The power struggle escalates. One or more of the children now cries louder or yells at the parent or throws a stuffed animal. It gets late. The children wander out of bed to find their parents. They are told to go back to bed, but they don't want to. They want to hang out on the couch, or they want to sleep in their parents' bed. The parents feel helpless and exhausted. They look at each other until one of them finally says, "Okay, you can sleep in our bed with us, just this one night." And so it begins—the start of the co-sleeping habit.

The children in this scenario are not babies. They may be three, five, seven, ten years old, or any age. Their parents are reluctant, reactive co-sleepers who feel overwhelmed and get to the point of believing they have no choice but to co-sleep. But they do have a choice.

Like other habits, the co-sleeping habit is insidious. It starts slowly and, over time, becomes deeply entrenched, and ends up having a negative impact on the well-being of everyone in the household.

As with other habits, you may have attempted to change it, perhaps when the children were toddlers, or when they were older. A co-sleeping habit based on your being worn down is not what your children need. If your co-sleeping is like this, you are a reactive co-sleeper rather than a parent co-sleeping based on a philosophy or plan.

If you are co-sleeping out of habit, inertia, or guilt, if co-sleeping causes problems in your marriage, or if you feel you are confusing your child's needs with your own, then you are ready to set better bedtime boundaries and teach your children how to sleep without you.

You are in the co-sleeping habit if you:

- Fall asleep in your child's bed because your child insists that you lie down and then pitches a fit when you try to get up and leave the room.
- Go through a whole bedtime routine with the intention of your children sleeping in their own beds, but when they cry, beg, and keep leaving their beds, you give in and bring them into your bed—or you sleep with them in the family room or somewhere else in the house.

The bottom line of reactive co-sleeping is that you co-sleep with your child or children because you give in to their insistence that they be with you during some part or all through the night. When you engage in reactive co-sleeping as a regular routine because you decide to skip the dreaded power struggle, you have crossed the line from reactive co-sleeping into the co-sleeping habit.

Do you ever say to yourself, "Why go through all of this carrying on? I'll just sleep with them." If your children control you at night, it is likely that they control you during the day. This means that you allow your children to make decisions that you should be making.

Being reactive to your children's behavior is not the same as being responsive to their needs. Being responsive means that you are in tune with your child so that when your child overreacts, for example by crying hysterically when there is no danger, you take that as a signal to come up with a plan that will teach your child how to feel and function better. Your goal as a responsive parent is to encourage your child to cope, not to just react by stopping the crying with an action that leads nowhere.

Sometimes reactive co-sleeping starts with intentional co-sleeping. You may have planned to try the family bed, or the co-sleeping philosophy underlying attachment parenting, and then changed your mind. But your children didn't change their minds, and now you feel stuck because they really like the co-sleeping.

Just remember that parenting is a form of leadership. If you decide that it is time to encourage and teach your children how to sleep independently because you believe it would be in the best interest of your children and your family, you can learn how to make that change. You can guide your children based on your intimate knowledge of how they think and function. Your decisions as a parent should be intentional, not reactive.

Intentional parents are responsive to their children's needs, not reactive to their children's demands. Intentional parenting is based on your evaluation of how to meet your children's needs and maintain balance within your family. Your children need you to be less reactive and more responsive and intentional. This means getting perspective and taking the time to think about what might be driving their nighttime behavior. You know your children better than anyone. Maybe they resist bedtime because they need more time with you or your spouse during the day. Maybe your children need to learn coping skills so that they can sleep without you. Their nighttime behavior has become a habit that they can change with your help.

No matter how long you and your children have been in the co-sleeping habit and no matter how old your children are, you can break the co-sleeping habit and teach your children how to sleep independently. Rather than rewarding your children for winning a power struggle, you can learn how to make a plan that will teach your children how to cope with bedtime and independent sleep. You can learn to follow through and achieve your goal of everyone sleeping in his or her own bed. This book will show you how.

As a licensed psychologist, I have provided parent education and family therapy for more than twenty-five years. I have helped parents change long-standing patterns that have thwarted their goals. I have found that the co-sleeping habit is widespread.

In preparation for this book, I did a survey of parents who were in the waiting room at two pediatricians' offices in the fall of 2007, bringing in their children for office visits that had nothing to do with the co-sleeping issue. The ages of their children ranged from two through fourteen years. I found that of the parents who co-sleep with their children (more than half), two-thirds of these parents circled yes on a survey to the question: Do you let your children control the sleep arrangement because they scream, cry, or demand to be with you at night? Therefore, the majority of parents in this survey who co-sleep were not doing so based on a well-thought-out parenting plan.

Notice the ages. These children are not babies. Their parents are reactive co-sleepers who engage in the co-sleeping habit because they feel controlled by their children—not because co-sleeping is based on an attachment parenting plan. What do you suppose happens when these same children—toddlers through teens—scream, cry, or demand their parents to give in to them during the day? The more demanding these children are, the louder they carry on, the more control they obtain over these weary parents—night and day.

When you break this habit and sleep becomes normalized, there are meaningful, positive changes in the functioning of all family members, not only at nighttime, but during the day as well.

I have found that parents who teach their children—toddlers through teens—coping skills at night have seen positive changes in their children's daytime behavior.

Many parents have told me they wish their baby had popped out with a manual. If a manual had been part of the package, it would say:

- If you are co-sleeping with your child out of habit, stop.
- Breaking the co-sleeping habit and teaching your children how to sleep in their own beds can:
  - Improve the quality of sleep for you and your children
  - Reduce your children's fears at night
  - Teach your children coping skills
  - Give your children confidence to deal with new challenges during the day
  - Teach your children the value of privacy
  - Strengthen your bond with your partner
  - Improve your relationship with your children
- The manual would go on to say:
  - There's hope. No matter how long you have engaged in the co-sleeping habit, you can change it. As with any other habit, change requires motivation, knowledge, support, and follow-through with a plan that you can maintain.

Let this book be your manual for breaking the co-sleeping habit. This book will provide you with the tools you need to extricate you and your children, toddlers through teenagers, from this nighttime behavior pattern. Remedies for breaking the co-sleeping habit include learning the value of calm, assertive leadership, learning how to overcome your inner barriers to making the necessary changes, and learning how to set appropriate limits and boundaries for sleep while maintaining strong parent-child connections. Families who learn how to be connected without being either overinvolved or disengaged function well and contain family members who flourish as individuals.

You will be taken through a journey that can have a profoundly positive impact on your children's current behavior, the quality of their sleep, the quality of your sleep, your children's emotional stability and relationships now and in the future, the health of your marriage, and the well-being of your family.

How This Book Works

The book is divided into three parts. Throughout this book, you will learn about the benefits of independent sleep for your children and family and how to achieve this goal. All anecdotes and cases throughout the book are actually blends of different people and families. Details were changed and fictitious names were used.

Part I, Staying Attached Without Co-Sleeping, will explain what attachment is all about, how it is maintained, and that it is not the same as co-sleeping. You will be given the opportunity to understand and evaluate your particular co-sleeping situation and will be shown the many benefits of independent sleep, including positive changes in your children's daytime behavior.

Part II, How to Break the Co-Sleeping Habit, will guide you on becoming a calm, assertive leader in your home, will take you step-by-step in challenging mental barriers that have prevented you from breaking the co-sleeping habit in the past, and will show you how to break the co-sleeping habit at every age level, toddlers through teens, regardless of how the habit started or how long it has gone on.

Part III, A Closer Look at Families in the Co-Sleeping Habit, will bring to life a variety of forms that the co-sleeping habit takes when it has started well after infancy has ended. This part of the book tells the stories of "families" in which parents and children are in the co-sleeping habit. Each family is really a blend of lots of families with names and details changed. As you read the stories, see if you identify with any of the families described. Tips are provided for addressing each form of the co-sleeping habit.

The conclusion of the book will give you the opportunity to evaluate how far you have come in breaking the co-sleeping habit.

Part I

Staying Attached Without Co-Sleeping

This part of the book will explain what attachment is all about and how you can set bedtime boundaries and establish and maintain a secure attachment with your children at the same time.

You will have the opportunity to examine why you are co-sleeping and decide if the co-sleeping in your house is part of an attachment plan, or if you are co-sleeping with your children out of habit. You will also see how breaking the co-sleeping habit can increase your children's daytime confidence, decrease manipulation and interrupting, and help your children cope better with transitions night and day.

CHAPTER 1

Attachment During Infancy and Beyond

Do you feel worn down because it takes hours to get your children to go to sleep? Are you exhausted because you sleep with your toddler? Your four-year-old? How about your seven- or nine-year-old? Your teenager?

Was it your intention to co-sleep with your children who are no longer infants, or did co-sleeping become a habit that is now out of control?

Maybe it was your plan to co-sleep with your infant, but when you decided to shift to independent sleep, your child had different ideas. Now you are so drained from bedtime power struggles that you have allowed co-sleeping to become a habit instead of a plan.

If you are co-sleeping with your children out of habit, out of guilt, or because you feel like your children give you no choice, you need to get on a different path. You can get your child out of your bed, or get out of your child's bed, without hurting the attachment between you and your child. In fact, co-sleeping is not necessary for secure parent-child attachment, even in infancy.

Attachment and Co-Sleeping Are Not the Same Thing

Attachment is the quality of relationship between parents and children and is accomplished by being responsive to children's needs starting at birth and through their development as their needs change. It is the love relationship between parent and child that helps shape a child into a secure, happy person who feels valuable and self-confident.

Touch and affection are essential to secure attachment. Your growing child needs to be cuddled, stroked, hugged, and comforted with physical reassurances. However, the physical part of attachment can be accomplished throughout the day, without co-sleeping. Loving touch is an important component of the parent-child relationship, not only during infancy but also throughout development.

Establishing and maintaining attachment with your child involves more than physical closeness. Attachment parenting is accomplished by your making the choice to strive for a high-quality and balanced parent-child relationship.

You don't have to make the conscious choice to co-sleep with your children to create secure attachment or to ensure that attachment lasts. In fact, there are some circumstances in which co-sleeping, even with your infant, works against your attachment goal. For example, Dr. William Sears, the pediatrician who coined the term *attachment parenting*, cautions against confusing legitimate adult needs with the needs your parents didn't meet for you when you were a child. You also need to consider balancing your child's needs with your marriage, your personal preferences, and the quality of your sleep as a primary caregiver who needs to be refreshed.

Many parents express the misconception that attachment parenting is all about co-sleeping. Some parents believe that they must wait until the child decides it's time to stop co-sleeping and that teaching a child how to sleep without the parent is inappropriate or even cruel. Some of you may have even felt peer pressure from parents who believe that co-sleeping, or sleep sharing, is the only right way to ensure your child's security and healthy development. But the touching and physical closeness do not have to extend into a co-sleeping arrangement.

Many people who never co-slept with their parents have secure attachments with them and are happy, well-functioning adults, partners, and parents themselves. There are also many people who grew up co-sleeping with their parents but did not develop secure attachments with them and now have difficulty in their current relationships.

All Infants Are Insecure Because They Are Infants

Insecurity is natural in infancy because infants cannot take care of themselves. They cannot survive without someone else meeting their needs. To ensure survival, healthy infants come equipped with the survival tools of instinctive crying and large lung capacity. These tools allow infants to cry out to a caregiver to help them, comfort them, and feed them.

When you respond to your infant's cries during the day as well as the night, you send positive messages that help build trust and confidence. You are showing your infant that he or she is loved and valued.

Experts in child development agree that it is important to be sensitive to and respond to your infant's needs for comfort and protection. Secure attachment early in infancy allows the older infant and young child to have the self-confidence to adapt to the new, unfamiliar situations that are part of growing up.

Although many parents establish secure, lasting attachment with their infant in a crib from the start, others believe strongly in establishing a family bed to provide their infant with physical closeness throughout the night.

The Family Bed

The concept of the family bed, or sleep sharing between parents and their children, originated in Eastern cultures. It had been part of Western cultures until the early 1900s for economic reasons.

After a long absence in Western culture, the family bed became popular again in the 1980s, when the practice of breastfeeding became widespread once again and mothers were encouraged to breastfeed their children through toddlerhood or even longer.

Sleep sharing makes breastfeeding during the night easier for both mother and child, whose sleep would not be disturbed the way it would if the mom had to get out of bed and wake up the baby in the crib. It also provides infants with close proximity and physical touch as an extension of daytime touching. In some cases, the family bed arrangement allows the sleep rhythms between parent and baby to become synchronized. But sleep sharing is not for everyone.

Even though sleep sharing can be an extension of daytime attachment parenting, this sleep arrangement is not a necessity for secure attachment, even in infancy.

One downside to the family bed is that the child may never be willing to leave. Although some children make the decision for independent sleep on their own and within the same timeframe that you are hoping for, in many cases, the transition from the family bed to independent sleep is difficult for children—and it can be extremely difficult for you to convince your child to make the change. It's a good idea to have an exit plan in place from the start so that you can switch to independent sleep when it makes sense for you, your partner, or your children.

Another issue to consider is that the family bed limits private adult time—private conversation and lovemaking. Not all experts agree that it is okay to make love with your partner while your infant is in the bed. As your child gets older and remains in your bed for sleeping, you can make a plan for lovemaking somewhere outside the bedroom. However, given most people's schedules and the logistics in many homes, this idea may be hard to implement. Parents spending quality, private time together is good for the marriage and the soul. If you don't find a way to balance the family bed with private adult time, you might weaken the marriage bond and weaken the stability of your family unit. If this happens, the security of your child will automatically be threatened.

If you believe in the family bed for personal or cultural reasons or you are sleep sharing with your baby based on an attachment parenting plan, remember that sleep sharing only works when both parents support the arrangement. If one parent insists on sleep sharing over the objections of the other parent, co-sleeping as an attachment tool is misunderstood and can hurt the family. Even though everyone agrees that touch is essential for children and is good for parents, physical closeness and touch can be achieved without your children sleeping in your bed. So don't guilt-trip your partner into it.

When Only One of You Wants a Family Bed

Marie routinely slept with her parents, Carol and John, in their queen-size bed since she was born. Sleep sharing was planned, but by only one of her parents. After Marie's third birthday, her parents started marriage counseling. Both of these parents wanted to make a fresh start in their relationship. During the first two years of their marriage, before Marie was born, Carol and John felt connected and were hopeful about the future. They were health conscious people who enjoyed taking long walks, cooking meals together, and visiting with friends and family. They made love several times a week.

When Carol became pregnant, the couple's relationship changed. She was more enthusiastic about having a baby than he was. She became involved in reading baby and child rearing books, and he became more involved with work. Carol decided that sleep sharing would be the best way to stay attached to both her baby and her husband.

Mom Pressured Dad into Establishing a Family Bed

Before Marie was born, Carol interviewed pediatricians and established a relationship with one who supported sleep sharing. When eight months pregnant, Carol told John that establishing a family bed would make breastfeeding during the night easier, would make the baby feel secure, and would make them closer as a family. When he asked her how long the child would share a bed with them, she told him that they would all share a bed until the child was two years old. His jaw dropped.

She told her husband they had to do it for their baby and for their marriage. She implied that if he didn't go along with it, he wasn't father material and he didn't care about their marriage. John felt cornered, so he reluctantly agreed.

Can a Family Bed Heal a Marriage?

This mom thought it could. But the answer is no. Sleep sharing, or creating a family bed, is about meeting a child's needs. Neither sleep sharing nor the child should ever be used to fix an adult problem.

Carol hoped that having the family sleep together in the same bed would re-establish the bond Carol had lost with her husband. The idea backfired.

At first, John tried to feel good about the sleep sharing, but it wasn't working for him. He missed the nighttime privacy with his wife and didn't sleep as well with an infant in the bed. After two months, he asked Carol to agree to buy a crib for Marie. She wouldn't consider it. She told John that the idea of Marie waking up and seeing bars around her was horrible. She would not even hear of moving Marie into a crib in their room. Rather than bringing Carol and John closer together, having the baby in the bed deepened the divide between them.

Time moved on. By Marie's first birthday, John started to come home later. Carol accused him of having an affair, but this was not the case. He was working longer hours and getting lost in his computer as he felt more and more left out.

Carol reacted to his not taking to the family bed as a rejection of both her and the child. The family became out of balance.

When Marie turned age two, John reminded Carol that she had said they would move away from the family bed at this age. Carol didn't think Marie was ready. She was a clingy child who didn't interact with the other toddlers in the playgroup. Marie displayed separation anxiety by crying her heart out when Carol went to the bathroom at home, even if John was playing with her. Carol told him there is no way that their child was ready to sleep without them. When he asked her when Marie would be ready, Carol told him she didn't know. And she wanted another baby. He stopped making love with his wife. However, he did continue to participate in the family bed arrangement because he was afraid that if he didn't, it might mean he was a bad father.

By the time Marie was three years old, John and Carol were barely speaking. One day after Marie's third birthday party, John gave Carol an ultimatum—either Marie will learn to sleep in her own bed, or he will be sleeping elsewhere. This was when marriage counseling began.

Moving from Sleep Sharing to Independent Sleep

Early in the marriage counseling it came to light that there were problems in Carol and John's marriage before Marie was born. This couple hadn't really discussed having a child. Sleep sharing with Marie was not a joint decision. John felt coerced into it. Carol felt rejected by his not wanting the family bed. Although the past cannot be changed, this marriage could move forward and be healed with improved communication and a re-establishment of trust. First, the child had to be taken out of the middle, both figuratively and literally.

John wanted his wife back. But he didn't want to look like the bad guy. He did not want to hurt his daughter by insisting she sleep alone.

Carol wanted her husband back. She was willing to see him as a loving parent even though he wanted to sleep without Marie.

They agreed to teach Marie how to sleep independently. The parents made a plan to work together and teach Marie how to sleep independently in her own space. They bought Marie a toddler bed, placed it in the second bedroom, which was now officially her bedroom, and brought her toys, stuffed animals, and clothes into the room. They decorated the room in colors and touches that they knew Marie would enjoy. Then they worked on helping Marie form positive associations with her new space during the day.

Carol and John supported each other in helping their daughter transition out of the family bed. They walked Marie through a bedtime routine that led to their tucking her in. They taught her how to self-comfort in her own bed. They told her gently, but clearly, that she did not need to be with them in the same bed anymore.

During the process, the couple's communication improved and their trust grew as they noticed each other acting as loving parents. They also noticed that Marie became more confident. She enjoyed, for the first time, playing by herself while someone was nearby, rather than having to have the adult play with her all the time. She separated more easily to play with her peers. Her parents gave her lots of hugs and kisses and praise. They took pride in her emerging independence and began to understand what attachment parenting is really all about, that you have to be flexible in how you meet your child's needs and that closeness with a child is not supposed to come between you.

For some families, the family bed or sleep sharing can be a successful part of an attachment parenting plan. In this family, in which attachment parenting and the spirit of sleep sharing were misunderstood, the family bed turned out to be disastrous for the marriage and almost destroyed it.

Co-Sleeping and the Family Bed

- Do not impose the family bed on your partner.
- Remember that co-sleeping is not a necessity for attachment.
- Think through the decision carefully.
- Have an exit plan worked out in advance in case you change your mind.
- Co-sleeping is not a substitute for spending quality time with your child during the day.
- Never use the family bed to fix a troubled marriage.

Maintaining Your Marriage

Keeping your marriage strong will provide your children with stability. If co-sleeping interferes with the quality of your relationship with your spouse, then co-sleeping will not be good for your children.

The same holds true in blended families. If you are remarried and your spouse is uncomfortable with co-sleeping, or if you are lying down next to your child in another room night after night, falling asleep while waiting for your three-year-old or eight-year-old to fall asleep, you are putting up a barrier in your partnership.

Your children's needs will not be met if their foundation crumbles because you and your significant other cannot agree about co-sleeping. If you force the issue of co-sleeping, you may find your partner resenting you or your child. If you share sleep with your child instead of your partner, you are creating an imbalance in the family that will not benefit any of you.

Maintaining Attachment after Infancy

It is your job to ensure that the bond between your child and you stays strong throughout life. So if co-sleeping isn't the answer, what can you do to promote and maintain secure parent-child attachment after infancy? Your attachment with your children is maintained through the quality of your relationship with them as they grow. As Dr. Sears has put it, remain emotionally responsive and meet your child's needs, recognizing that their needs will change over time.

Maintaining attachment is done by such things as listening when your children need to talk with you, enjoying your children's company, supporting them with guidance and affection when they are stressed or troubled about something, spending time with them doing the activities that they enjoy, allowing them to express their opinions, and having dinner together at the table more than just once in a while. It is also done by showing genuine interest in your children—attending school conferences and events, encouraging your children to make friends, showing an appreciation of their interests and accomplishments, and trying to see their point of view. If you're doing a good job, their opinions won't always match yours. They will feel comfortable expressing themselves.

Giving your children the tools and encouragement for coping with independent sleep by breaking the co-sleeping habit is one of the ways to maintain secure attachment with your child when infancy is over.

Encouraging Self-Comfort in Your Toddler

When your infant's needs are met consistently, the ability to cope or to self-comfort begins to develop. You can see coping skills begin to emerge when your toddler clutches a stuffed animal for comfort when he or she is upset or when you leave the room. The self-comforting behavior helps your toddler cope with normal separation.

Coping skills take time to unfold. If you give your toddler the opportunity to self-comfort, he or she will learn how to meet other needs with less help from you. As your children get older, they will become increasingly self-sufficient if you show them how to comfort themselves when they are younger.

By gently encouraging your toddler to use inner resources to cope with change and uncertainty, your child will grow into a secure and grounded adolescent and adult. However, if you treat your toddler and older child like a one-year-old, the seeds of coping will not be able to flower and your child could stay dependent and regressed. Separation anxiety, rather than diminishing the way it is supposed to, can increase.

This does not mean that you should ignore your child's needs or cries for help. It means that as the parent, it is your job to reveal to your children the magic that they have inside of them to deal with stressful situations, the magic that you helped them develop throughout infancy when they could do so little for themselves. Unlike the helpless infant, your toddler can walk instead of crawl, talk instead of babble, and drink out of a cup instead of a bottle. Your toddler can also imagine your face, voice, and touch—even when you're not present in the room. Thus, your toddler's knowledge and trust that you are in the house should be sufficient for coping with independent sleep.

Separation anxiety is normal for a one-year-old. At this age, your baby shows signs of discomfort in the presence of strangers or people he or she doesn't know well. It is important to help your baby to feel safe. Separation anxiety usually peaks at around age two, persists for a while, and then slowly diminishes. If you are as anxious as your toddler or older child when you separate, your child's separation anxiety may be prolonged.

Attachment Requires Shifting Gears as Your Child Develops

To maintain healthy attachment, you need to change what you do as a parent as your children's needs change. You can learn how to protect your growing children without overprotecting them from harmless situations.

If you create too much togetherness, you might hold them back from building on the bond you created in infancy. Dr. John Bowlby, who developed attachment theory, found that individuals who grow up to be stable and self-reliant usually have parents who are supportive when called upon but who also permit and encourage autonomy. Children who are securely attached in infancy can draw upon the internal representation of the attachment figure that they have in their minds to help themselves with autonomy.

Many well-meaning parents mistakenly view secure bonding as staying attached at the hip with their children, even older children—including throughout the night. If their children show any discomfort about sleeping independently, they react by co-sleeping rather than by teaching their children coping skills. This parental reactivity can trigger anxiety and make children act and feel like infants, not only at bedtime, but also during the day.

As parents, you need to stop viewing independent sleep for your children as exposure to a traumatic situation. Independent sleeping is a normal, safe, daily part of life, and learning how to cope with separation at bedtime is something children need to learn how to do, just as they must learn how to use the bathroom or how to share a toy.

Learning how to do all these things shows the ability to cope with new challenges that are part of growing up. The secure relationship known as attachment, which you establish with your children from the beginning, lays the foundation for their self-confidence and knowledge that they are safe to do certain things without you.

Raising a secure child when infancy is over requires knowing how much to hold on and how much to let go. If you hold on too tightly, instead of being securely bonded you and your children may be in bondage.

Staying Attached with Balanced Family Connections

Healthy families establish a balance between separateness and togetherness. You certainly don't want an unconnected family in which the bonds among family members are weak. In unconnected families, each person has little need of the others, not because of healthy independence but because of lack of emotional trust or intimacy. In unconnected families, there is little meaningful communication or nurturance.

However, you also don't want your family to be on the other end of the spectrum, where separateness isn't tolerated. When there's no separateness, families are considered enmeshed or over-involved. The boundaries between parent and child are blurred. You can't tell where one individual ends and the other begins.

Balanced connections make bonds stronger while, at the same time, allowing each family member to be an individual with his or her own personality. Balanced family connections promote feelings of security in children. Achieving a healthy balance in your connection with your children is an important part of your role as a parent.

Attachment Is Not Enmeshment

Attachment is a healthy goal. You cannot be too attached to your child if you understand that attachment is simply staying in tune with your growing child's needs. Attachment parenting allows children to grow into individuals in their own right. With this goal in mind, attached parents are perceptive of the signs of their children's emerging independence. Attached parents are responsive parents who teach their children how to meet their own needs and how to cope with change. Enmeshed parents, however, have difficulty separating their child's needs from their own. They think they are the same.

Enmeshed parents still function on the level of a child and try to get their unfulfilled childhood needs met by their own children. Enmeshed parents are not able to let their children grow up and are not able to adjust to their children's changing needs. Dr. Sears warns parents about the dangers of parents smothering the child emotionally, keeping the child from developing his or her own individual personality.

Many years ago, Dr. Salvador Minuchin, a renowned family therapist, distinguished enmeshed families from healthy families. Dr. Minuchin recognized that rather than promoting true closeness, enmeshment blurs the boundaries between people. It's as though you can't tell where one person ends and the other begins.

Rather than establishing a balance that includes both separateness and togetherness, the parents of enmeshed families are controlling and intrusive. In this type of parent-child relationship, communication is constricted and privacy is considered a rejection rather than a legitimate human need.

Children who are securely attached to their parents are equipped to face the challenge of developing into unique individuals who can balance togetherness with individuality. But children who are enmeshed with one or both parents have difficulty forming a clear sense of self and may develop insecurities in the face of life challenges and transitions.

Finding the Right Balance

In balanced families with securely attached children, parents make a clear distinction between who the adults are, who the children are, and how these roles are different. The adults are always the leaders of the family and should share a healthy bond with each other. When children control the household, the family becomes out of balance. Managing the family is not a burden young children should have, and it can lead to chaos in your household.

Parents who are calm, assertive leaders don't yell, scream, or beg when their children misbehave. They discipline their children without anger or desperation and do not give in to unreasonable demands. Finding the right balance means creating a plan that allows your children to thrive not only during the day, but also at bedtime and through the night as well. Parents who co-sleep with their children out of habit are diminishing their role as the leaders of the family and may fall prey to the pitfalls of overinvolvement.

The Pitfalls of Overinvolvement

Instead of creating true closeness, overinvolvement discourages the use of coping skills in children.

There's a downside for you as well. Parents who overidentify with their children are hesitant to set limits for their children's behavior and generally fail to follow through with discipline. Their children are either clingy or out of control. The lack of limits often is due to parents' fear that their children will not love them if they don't do everything their kids want. This misconception often results in chaos in the household and wreaks havoc on child development and marital relationships. The poor limit setting occurring during the day can extend into the night in the form of the co-sleeping habit.

Achieving and maintaining balanced family connections is a very important part of your role as a parent. By recognizing and changing your potential overinvolvement, you can make the shift to a more balanced connection that will allow your children to flourish.

How Overinvolvement Can Hurt Adolescents

The developmental task of adolescence is a balancing act. There needs to be less dependency on parents without sacrificing attachment relationships to parents. To perform this task successfully adolescents require a foundation of security and balanced family connections in which self-confidence and individuality have been fostered.

Well-intentioned parents who react to a child's nighttime anxiety with the co-sleeping habit can pave the way for insecurities down the road in adolescence. Take the case of Madeleine, a seventeen-year-old high school senior in the process of applying to college.

On the surface, Madeleine appeared to function well. She had a B average, a part-time job after school, and several close friends. Underneath, though, she suffered from anxiety bordering on panic. She was a good driver, but was terrified of driving on the highway. She would take any route possible to avoid highway driving. She was always pleasant to customers and coworkers at her job, but cried in the bathroom and felt depressed for hours if anyone criticized her at work.

Madeleine dreamed of being an artist, but the nearest fine arts college program was several hours from her home. As much as she wanted to apply, she didn't because attending would mean living away from home and then highway driving when coming home on weekends.

Madeleine's parents knew their daughter was easily stressed, and they comforted her with kind, encouraging words, but it did no good. She felt even more pressured when her dad would say, "You're so bright. You can become anything you want."

When Madeleine was five years old, facing kindergarten was difficult for her, and she sought comfort in her parents' bed. Her parents thought it was reasonable to let her sleep between them to ease her transition to starting school. Their son had never asked for this type of comfort, but Madeleine seemed more fragile than her brother.

As time went on, co-sleeping became a habit. Madeleine's dad would tuck her into her own bed, and to please him, she stayed there for a while. But she would remain awake, and after an hour or so, she would go into her parents' room, tug at her mother and say, "Mom, I'm scared. Could you come and sleep with me?" Her mother would get out of bed and curl up with her daughter in the child's bed and stay there all night, almost every night, all the way through high school.

Madeleine's mother, who grew up in a rather cold, unaffectionate household, felt that it would be mean to make her daughter sleep alone. Madeleine's father did not like that his wife slept with their daughter instead of with him, but he didn't know how to get them to change their co-sleeping habit. Neither parent saw the connection between this imbalance in the family and Madeleine's insecurities, fears, and low self-confidence that were narrowing her life.

For some families, overinvolvement between parents and their adolescent children leads to conflict. This can happen when parents interpret the adolescent's striving for identity as a threat to the parent-child relationship. Adolescents with overinvolved parents often feel judged for going through the confusing process of identity formation. Instead of seeing their parents as a secure base, these adolescents often become frustrated and alienated.

They feel their parents are not listening, but at the same time, they fear that challenging their parents directly will result in rejection. The increase in parent-adolescent conflict can lead to lying and prevent the enmeshed adolescent from relying on his or her parents as a safety net. The ability to develop a true sense of self can become impaired. Adolescents who have difficulty expressing their feelings in a healthy, straightforward way have poor decision-making skills and can be excessively needy. A highly developed sense of self allows teens to maintain secure and balanced relationships with their parents. If balanced family relationships, rather than overinvolvement, are established and maintained when children are younger, they can develop their independence and later as adolescents maintain a secure attachment with their parents.

The Bottom Line

If your children are afraid to sleep without you, you have an important parenting decision to make about how to help them handle the fear. If you feel guilty or afraid to find a better balance between separateness and togetherness, you may have gotten yourself and your children into the co-sleeping habit.

When you become confident that your children can learn to sleep through the night without you, they will internalize your confidence and make it their own. Rather than fear and exhaustion, you will project calm leadership in the family, which will enhance your children's emotional security.

Your co-sleeping habit may have started as an attempt to promote attachment or to reduce your children's fears, but now you realize you can stay attached without co-sleeping and show your children it is safe to sleep without you. By breaking the co-sleeping habit, you will find the right balance in your relationship with your children. You will see positive changes in their functioning, not only at bedtime but during the day as well.

To begin to address the particular balance issues in your family you must understand why you and your children are currently co-sleeping. The next chapter is designed to help you figure that out.

CHAPTER 2

Why Are You Co-Sleeping?

K nowing why you do the things you do is an important step toward making a change. Before breaking the
co-sleeping habit, you need to understand why you are
co-sleeping. Answering the questions in this chapter will help
you gain insight into the factors that are maintaining the co-
sleeping habit between you and your child.

Why Are You Co-Sleeping?
Your First Co-Sleep Quiz

There will be three co-sleep quizzes in this book. This first one
is designed to help you determine why you are co-sleeping. An
assumption underlying the quiz is that co-sleeping is not working
for your family. Therefore, the quiz is designed to identify the specific nature of your co-sleeping challenge rather than to consider
co-sleeping as an attachment tool that is effective for your family.

There are no right or wrong answers but there are truthful
and less truthful answers. So be honest with yourself. You can't
change something that you can't admit to yourself.

With all of this in mind, answer yes or no to each of the questions. Right after the quiz there is a brief discussion to help you
deepen your understanding of your co-sleeping habit.

Co-Sleep Quiz 1

Answer yes or no to each of these questions. If you can't decide, answer yes if it's mostly true, and answer no if it's mostly not true.

_____ 1. Do your children wear you down until you give in to co-sleeping?

_____ 2. Do you feel controlled by your children at bedtime?

_____ 3. Do you fall asleep in your child's bed while waiting for your child to fall asleep?

_____ 4. Do you "discover" your child in your bed in the middle of the night or in the morning?

_____ 5. Do you find yourself playing "musical beds" at night because your child won't fall asleep or stay asleep?

_____ 6. Did your child have an illness that required co-sleeping, and now your child is better but won't sleep without you?

_____ 7. Have you tried but not been able to change from co-sleeping to independent sleep?

_____ 8. Do you worry that your children will be mad at you if you stop co-sleeping?

_____ 9. Are you co-sleeping to make up for being too busy for your child during the day?

_____ 10. Are you co-sleeping with your children to comfort yourself?

_____ 11. Are you co-sleeping to protect your child from feelings of rejection you suffered as a child?

_____ 12. Does one parent sleep with your child and the other parent sleeps somewhere else?

_____ 13. Do you and your partner disagree about co-sleeping?

_____ 14. Are you avoiding your spouse or partner by co-sleeping with your child?

If you answered yes to any of the first seven questions, then you are in the co-sleeping habit based on reactive co-sleeping rather than on a parenting plan.

Yes to Question 1

Do your children wear you down until you give in to co-sleeping?

If your children wear you down until you give in, you are a reactive co-sleeper who co-sleeps out of habit, not based on a conscious choice. You are co-sleeping because it is the path of least resistance. Your co-sleeping is not based on a plan or on your intention to engage in attachment parenting. Rather than responding to your children's behavior as a signal that you need to work with them on their coping skills, you are taking the easy way out. You are letting them be in charge of you. You may be inadvertently giving them the message that manipulation will get them what they want, not only at bedtime, but during the day as well.

Yes to Question 2

Do you feel controlled by your children at bedtime?

If you feel controlled by your children at bedtime, you need to learn how to become a calm, assertive leader in your home. Co-sleeping is currently dictated by your children. Ask yourself if you allow your children to make other child rearing decisions as well. Be responsive to your children's needs, but don't let them be in charge. Being in charge of an adult and a household may make your children feel powerful in the moment, but in the long run, this is a burden for children. In spite of their behavior, children really want the adults in the family to be in charge of the family.

Yes to Question 3

Do you fall asleep in your child's bed while waiting for your child to fall asleep?

If you fall asleep in your child's bed while waiting for your child to fall asleep, you have clearly fallen prey to the co-sleeping habit. The chances are this habit began when your child would not "let" you leave after being tucked in. You can learn how to tuck in more effectively so that your child learns how to cope with, and even enjoy, the privacy of the presleep period.

Yes to Question 4

Do you "discover" your child in your bed in the middle of the night or in the morning?

Parents have told me that they "discover" their child in their bed some time in the night or in the morning, having never realized that their child entered their room, much less their bed. If this is your co-sleeping issue, then it is surely a habit. You are so used to having another person come into your bed, you don't even notice that it's happening. This is a passive form of night-time parenting and not a conscious choice or plan. It turns out that some parents do actually sense that the child has come into the bed, but they are too tired to escort the child back or don't want to deal with the protest.

Yes to Question 5

Do you find yourself playing "musical beds" at night because your child won't fall asleep or stay asleep?

If you find yourself playing "musical beds" at night because your child won't fall asleep or stay asleep, you are encouraging poor sleep habits. Playing musical beds can take the form of your moving from one child's bed to another in your attempt to get your children to go to sleep, your moving your children in and out of your room in your attempt to get them to sleep, or your moving with your children from their beds, to the sofa, to the sleeping bag, and all over the place through the night to get them to sleep. Playing musical beds is not based on a plan. It is chaotic and allows no one in the house to get a good night's sleep. You and your children are most likely sleep deprived from this form of the co-sleeping habit.

Yes to Question 6

Did your child have an illness that required co-sleeping, and now your child is better but won't sleep without you?

If your child had an illness that required co-sleeping and now is better but won't sleep without you, your co-sleeping used to be based on a conscious plan, but now it is not. It has become a habit. If your child's pediatrician or specialist has assured you that it is safe for your child to sleep without you but you continue to co-sleep because your child has gotten so comfortable with co-sleeping that he or she wants it to be a continuing or permanent arrangement, then you are a reactive co-sleeper. Of course, you and your partner can make the choice that co-sleeping continues to benefit the family even though your child is now well. But if it is the case that your child refuses to sleep without you even though you want to go back to separate sleeping, then you can take logical steps in a nurturing way to break the co-sleeping habit.

Yes to Question 7

Have you tried but not been able to change from co-sleeping to independent sleep?

If you have tried but have not been able to change from co-sleeping to independent sleep, then you already know you are in the co-sleeping habit. Habits can be hard to break, even when you have clear intentions. If you have tried unsuccessfully, then you have let your children wear you down or you have given in to physical and emotional exhaustion. Maybe you have had difficulty with following through with a plan to change from co-sleeping to independent sleep. Maybe you simply gave up. Until now.

The answer yes to Questions 8, 9, 10, or 11 indicates that emotional reasoning and your own needs are maintaining the co-sleeping habit at your house.

Yes to Question 8

Do you worry that your children will be mad at you if you stop co-sleeping?

If you are worried that your child will be mad at you or won't love you anymore or as much if you break the co-sleeping habit, co-sleeping may be stemming from your own insecurities. You need to have more faith in your value as a parent and in your child's attachment to you. Although your child may become angry when you change a routine that has been longstanding, it is important that you don't live in fear of your child's anger or be ruled by it.

Change is uncomfortable for children, as it is for adults. Breaking a habit is difficult. Anger can be a protest about the discomfort of change. But change is a part of life. It is up to you to teach your child how to deal with change. By helping your child adapt to a new routine, the discomfort will pass and independent sleep will then become comfortable. The love your child has for you will not dissipate as you teach him or her to cope with change and learn new skills. If this were really an issue, then parents wouldn't guide their children to do anything differently from the way they want to do them and children would raise themselves.

Yes to Question 9

Are you co-sleeping to make up for being too busy for your child during the day?

If you are co-sleeping to make up for being too busy for your child during the day, you need to think about how you can make some changes and manage your time differently during the day. It is during the day that most attachment parenting takes place. It is during the day that your child talks with you about school, about friends, about accomplishments, and about self-doubt. It is during the day that you can share your child's interests and show pride in his or her accomplishments. Sitting with your child before bed is a valuable time for sharing—but bed sharing after tucking in does not compensate for too little daytime contact. Co-sleeping is not a solution for making up for time you spend working or doing chores. If you feel guilty for not spending enough quality time with your children while they are awake, then do whatever you can to change it.

Yes to Question 10

Are you co-sleeping with your children in order to comfort yourself?

It is not your child's role to comfort you during the night. In fact, it is not your child's responsibility to make you feel better about anything. Divorce can make you feel lonely and so can sleeping alone while your spouse is at work. But if you burden your children with your needs, they may feel overwhelmed. Some children develop a sense of failure because of being unable to fill a void in their parents' lives or hearts. Some children crave their own personal space for sleep but are afraid their parent won't be okay sleeping without them. In this case, the co-sleeping habit can create what is called a parentified child, an overburdened child who acts like your parent instead of like your child. This role confusion can have a negative impact on your child's developing sense of self and future relationships. It can also undermine your authority.

Yes to Question 11

Are you co-sleeping to protect your child from feelings of rejection you suffered as a child?

If you feel that you were emotionally neglected, misunderstood, or rejected by your own parents or caregivers, it is important not to overcompensate by smothering your children. If you do, you will limit opportunities for your children to develop self-comforting and other coping skills. You want your children to be raised by the wisest, healthiest part of yourself, not by your wounded inner child. Challenge yourself. Make sure that you are not expecting your children to make you feel better about yourself. Also consider that you may be assuming that teaching your children to sleep without you will make them feel neglected or rejected. They may not feel that way. If you were not treated with respect as a child, you will most likely make sure that you will be caring and loving when teaching your children how to cope with the transition to bedtime.

If you answered yes to Question 12, 13, or 14, the co-sleeping habit is interfering in your marriage or relationship with your partner. Co-sleeping does not make children more secure if it hurts anyone's relationships in the family.

Yes to Question 12

Does one parent sleep with your child and the other parent sleeps somewhere else?

If you sleep with your child and your partner sleeps somewhere else (or if your partner sleeps with your child and you sleep somewhere else), there is an imbalance in the family that is not benefiting anyone. This type of imbalance can give your child the message that he or she is your peer. Your child might even think that he or she is responsible for problems in your marriage.

Yes to Question 13

Do you and your partner disagree about co-sleeping?

It is not unusual for partners to disagree about the co-sleeping issue. The important thing to keep in mind is that co-sleeping is neither right nor wrong. It's just right for some adults and children and not for others. So if you and your partner disagree about co-sleeping, there is no need to prove who is right. You just need to communicate openly until you work out your differences. If you co-sleep with your child over your partner's protests, or if you coerce your partner into sleep sharing, then co-sleeping will not benefit anyone involved. Children in this situation can feel as though they are coming between their parents and that the disagreement and deteriorating relationship between the parents is their fault.

Yes to Question 14

Are you avoiding your spouse or partner by co-sleeping with your child?

If you are avoiding your spouse or partner by co-sleeping with your child, you are using your child in a destructive way. This motive might be hard to admit to yourself, but if there is truth to it, you owe it to yourself, your children, and your spouse to deal with your marital issues without putting your children in the middle.

Now that you have taken Co-Sleep Quiz 1 and have gone over the explanations of your yes answers, you have a better understanding of why you are co-sleeping. You can see that the co-sleeping habit develops for a lot of different reasons and it can take many forms.

Whatever the reason for the existence of this habit in your household, remember that shifting to independent sleep has benefits for both you and your children. In addition to everyone getting better quality sleep and more sleep, you will help your children cope with the natural transition from day to night, you will help your children build their self-confidence, you will have more privacy, and your children will feel safe and secure seeing you as a confident, loving leader.

The benefits to breaking the co-sleeping habit and establishing independent sleep are not just about what happens at nighttime. The next chapter will show you further benefits of independent sleep that extend into the daytime.

CHAPTER 3

Further Benefits of Independent Sleep

For many generations, experts have debated the benefits of independent sleep versus co-sleeping and the consequences of sleep arrangements on children's daytime functioning. In fact, the controversy surrounding whether or not to co-sleep with your children is intense. Perhaps you have been bombarded by the opinions of well-meaning relatives and friends. Maybe you and your spouse don't see eye to eye on this issue. If you have tried to sort it out by seeing what the experts think, you may be even more confused.

In your search for the "right" answer, have you found that experts don't agree with each other? One day you come across an article whose author thinks that co-sleeping is a terrible idea, and the next morning you see a segment of a TV show with an expert explaining why it's healthy and natural.

Some experts believe that the family bed or sleep sharing will enhance the quality of the parent-child relationship and that making the conscious decision to co-sleep until the child expresses the desire to have his or her own bed is good practice. Other experts believe that independent sleep is an important step in child development and that parents should teach their children in a planned, consistent way to sleep in their own beds, even if this means that both parent and child undergo distress initially.

These conflicting opinions can overwhelm you even further. Let's look more closely at some of the expert opinions, starting with Dr. Benjamin Spock.

Dr. Spock

Dr. Spock was the most trusted expert in child development of the twentieth century. He was a pediatrician, psychoanalyst, and professor of child development. His most famous book, *Baby and Child Care,* was first published in 1946, has gone through seven editions, and has been translated into more than thirty languages. This book, which has sold over 50 million copies, has been referred to as the bible of child rearing for the parents of babies born after World War II—the baby boomers.

Why was Dr. Spock so popular? In addition to providing a wealth of readable child care information that was based on common sense, he focused on the emotional needs of children, parents, and families. He gave parents permission to cuddle their children and to pick up their babies in response to crying. The generation prior to Dr. Spock thought this was a bad idea and that the crying would be reinforced.

Regarding sleep, Dr. Spock believed that children are capable of sleeping in their own room by themselves from the time they are born as long as their parents are near enough to hear them when they cry. If the parents co-sleep with the baby, his recommendation was that children be out of their parents' room by age six months because if they haven't been moved by then, they may have set ideas where they want to sleep and it might be harder to get them to sleep independently.

He believed that if you react to your child's repeated attempts to get into your bed or to lie down with him or her, you are probably making a mistake and that it is better to put your child back to bed promptly and matter-of-factly, comforting the child that there is nothing to fear as you sit in a chair near the child's bed—not in the child's bed. With the exception of an acute illness, Dr. Spock thought it was a sensible rule not to take a child into a parent's bed to sleep.

Dr. Spock advised parents to be kind, but firm, at bedtime and to be willing to decide certain basic matters of management for their children's happiness as well as their own. He explained that parents should be responsive to their children's cries but not react by automatically co-sleeping to stop the child from crying. He believed that giving in to children's manipulations would lead to an increase in separation anxiety.

Dr. Spock's intention was to provide advice that would benefit and respect both children and their parents. Although Dr. Spock's opinions go back to the 1940s, many current experts agree with his observations and recommendations regarding parenting and children's sleep. Perhaps the best advice he gave parents was to have confidence in themselves. He said, "Trust yourself—You know more than you think you do."

Dr. Sears

An expert who may be better known to today's parents of young children is Dr. William Sears, the pediatrician who coined the term attachment parenting. Dr. Sears's attachment parenting approach is based on his interpretation of Dr. John Bowlby's attachment theory.

Dr. Sears views parenting as a twenty-four-hour-a-day job. However, he does not mean by this that you must be physically attached to your child all day and night. Although Dr. Sears believes that co-sleeping, or sleep sharing as Dr. Sears calls it, is desirable and can enhance attachment, he does not view co-sleeping as a requirement for secure parent-child attachment. In fact, Dr. Sears emphasizes that if sleep sharing is not working for you, your spouse, or your child, you should feel free to try other sleep arrangements.

Co-sleeping works for some children and their parents but not for others. He reassures mothers that they are not less of a mother if they don't sleep with their baby.

The emphasis in attachment parenting is on being emotionally available and cognizant of how your actions affect your children's well-being. Working mothers can be successful at attachment parenting.

Although experts may differ on the strategies they suggest, what the experts have in common is their commitment to healthy child development. The experts also agree that your parenting decisions should be intentional, based on a plan, a conscious choice. They think that your sleeping plan should be designed to help your children feel good about themselves, both now and in the future as they grow up, that it is up to you as parents to help your children feel secure. Experts would agree that your reacting impulsively in the moment, finding yourself entrenched in a habit, or fulfilling one family member's need at the expense of another does not fit with their suggestions regarding how and where children should sleep. You should look at the big picture—the family—and not just the child when making the decision about co-sleeping.

Unfortunately, some parents have taken the opinions of experts to extremes. Rather than acknowledging other parents' right to make the best decision for their child and their family, a judgmental, harsh tone has entered into the debate, pitting parents against each other and making some feel inadequate regarding their nighttime parenting choice. The important thing is to make a choice and not let your children, or other parents, take away your leadership role in your family.

Daytime Benefits of Independent Sleep

In addition to your children and the entire household functioning better at bedtime and through the night when you set bedtime boundaries, there are daytime benefits as well. Breaking the co-sleeping habit will provide a foundation for raising a secure, happy, well-adjusted child.

If you think about it, it makes sense that how you parent at night will have an impact on how your children feel about themselves and how they behave both night and day. If your children feel safe sleeping without you, they will feel safe facing other challenges without your having to be in their line of vision. When you give your children positive messages about their ability to cope and to self-soothe during the night, they have the opportunity to internalize and generalize these messages to feeling safe and secure during the day. They will feel more confident and secure when facing daytime challenges such as separating from you for school and social events.

When your children learn how to cope without intruding into your bedroom in the middle of the night, their new nighttime skills will generalize to less interrupting during the day.

If you do not accept manipulation and whining at bedtime, your children will find healthier ways to communicate their needs and desires not only at bedtime but also during the day. If you teach your children how to make a smoother transition to bedtime and sleep, they will have the opportunity to transfer these skills to making better transitions between activities during their day.

This does not mean that the minute your children sleep independently their daytime behavior will improve the next day. Children's daytime behaviors have become habits in their own right. However, there is a nighttime-daytime connection. Let's take a closer look at the further benefits of independent sleep that are in the fabric of the nighttime-daytime connection:

- Increased confidence
- Less interrupting
- Respect for privacy
- Less manipulation
- Smoother transitions

Increased Confidence

Shifting from the co-sleeping habit to independent sleep will give your children the opportunity for increased self-confidence not only at bedtime but also in their daytime pursuits. For children to gain confidence, they need to be empowered by the messages you give them at night as well as during the day.

If you "protect" your child from sleeping independently because you think it's just too hard for him or her to do it, your child can interpret your actions to mean: "You can't handle falling sleep. It's too hard for you." Your child can find the task of falling asleep without you difficult to accomplish because of internalizing these messages of helplessness surrounding the issue of sleep. Your child's nightly rehearsal of "I can't fall asleep" can generalize into "I can't" beliefs for daytime challenges as well.

Facing challenges, both big ones and small ones, can be overwhelming to a child who gets used to thinking, "I can't" or "It's too hard for me." Lack of confidence can stop children from trying new things and learning new skills, such as trying out for a sport or participating in class and risking giving the wrong answer.

You may have started sleep sharing to reduce your children's fears, but it turned out that your children began to exhibit fearful behavior and low self-confidence not only at bedtime but during the day as well. If your third grader, for example, says to herself night after night, "I'm not capable of falling asleep without my mom being right there with me," the same child is vulnerable to saying to herself when it's time to do homework, "I can't handle doing a math sheet all by myself. It's too hard for me."

You can increase your children's nighttime and daytime confidence by sending them empowering messages at bedtime. By setting bedtime boundaries, you will be telling your children, "You are capable of sleeping by yourself. You are safe and loved even when your parent is not right next to you." Many children transfer their nighttime empowerment into their daytime thinking and behavior.

Decreased Clinginess

Many parents who have not set bedtime boundaries have told me that their children are clingy not only at bedtime, but also during the day. They stick to you like glue.

Mothers in the co-sleeping habit with their toddlers have asked questions like: "Is it normal that my two-year-old hangs on to my leg while I'm making dinner? I have no choice but to drag him along when I move through the kitchen."

Parents who are in the co-sleeping habit with their kindergarteners have made statements like: "My daughter won't color unless I sit at the table with her. If I get up, she gets up and physically pulls me back. I can't reason with her that it's okay for her to color while I'm in the same room doing something else."

I remember more than one parent of children over age four who have told me, "They don't even let me go to the bathroom."

Even adolescents can be clingy. Does your fourteen-year-old son have to sit between the two of you on the sofa while you watch TV every night? Does your fifteen-year-old daughter hug you constantly, and even though this is a positive behavior, it seems too frequent?

Parents in the co-sleeping habit often notice their children clinging to them not only at home but also in social situations, even when their children know the people well. Clinging is not the same as shyness. Children who are shy may cling at first, but they do warm up to others and enter new situations when reassured. Clingy children act afraid in normal situations. A clingy child will hold on to you or hide behind you in situations when there is no threat.

If your children show fear of being a few feet away from you in safe situations where you are clearly available, how will they cope at a child's birthday party, at day camp, or with a baby sitter? In children who are toddlers through teens, clinginess in nonthreatening situations is not a measure of attachment. Rather, it is a reflection of their low self-confidence. If you help your children see that it is safe to sleep without you, they will feel safe to do other things without you.

You will find that boundaries at bedtime will lead to decreased clingy behavior when it's time to separate for sleep. Decreased clinginess at night goes hand and hand with more comfort with normal separations and increased confidence during the day.

Unless they are sick, there's an emergency, or there has been a prolonged separation, your children should be able to cope without having to physically touch you—at school or at a friend's house—and in their own bed.

Breaking the Cycle of Fear at Night

Everyone feels afraid from time to time. It's a normal human emotion. Without the ability to feel afraid, we wouldn't survive. Feeling afraid alerts you to danger and gives you the chance to save yourself from threat. But what if your child consistently perceives threat where there is none?

You can help your child be a better judge of true threat versus imagined threat. If you decrease your child's fears about sleeping without you, your child's daytime fears will diminish as well.

Let's look at what I call the cycle of fear:

- At bedtime, your child cries or begs you to stay.
- You interpret this to mean your child is frightened and needs you to stay.
- You react by engaging in the co-sleeping habit.
- Your child gets the message that sleeping alone is dangerous, maybe doing anything without you is dangerous, and maybe Mom and Dad are in danger, too.
- Your child is fearful during the day and imagines danger when there is none.
- At bedtime, your child cries or begs you to stay.
- You interpret this to mean your child is frightened and needs you to stay.
- You react by engaging in the co-sleeping habit . . . and so on.

If your child has demonstrated anxiety or worry during the day regarding situations where there really is no threat, you have probably tried saying something like, "There's nothing to be afraid of. You'll be okay." And it doesn't work. No matter how soothing your tone of voice is, your child won't be convinced. Your child may feel unsafe during the day, in spite of your soothing words, if your child feels it is unsafe to sleep without you through the night.

It's an uphill battle to teach your children to be confident and relaxed during the day if you are engaging in the co-sleeping habit at night. The messages and the beliefs that they have formed by your co-sleeping in reaction to their nighttime fears keep confirming that their fears are valid.

It's easier and more effective to intervene into the cycle of fear at night than it is during the day. For one thing, there are fewer distractions at night. The phone isn't ringing and you're not preparing a meal. Even though you're tired at night, you can motivate yourself by remembering that your efforts will show up not only in better sleep patterns for both you and your child, but also in increasing your child's daytime confidence.

Your children will be able to decrease their daytime fears and increase their self-confidence as they replace their fear-based thinking with the empowering messages you can communicate at bedtime by encouraging independent sleep.

When you consistently set bedtime boundaries, your children will interpret your new confidence in their ability to sleep independently as confidence in them. They will begin to realize that sleeping without you is safe and will generalize that doing other things without you—like visiting a friend's house or going to school—are safe, and that you, their parents, will be safe. You will decrease your child's worry habit so that he or she will be less fearful when there is no danger.

You will give your child the confidence and skills to go on life's journey with your guidance and support. This is what attachment parenting is really all about.

Less Interrupting

How many times have you heard yourself say, "Stop interrupting!" to your children? You have probably said this more times than you can remember.

Almost all children interrupt from time to time. Younger children have difficulty controlling themselves when they have something to say, so they just say it, even if you're talking on the phone, talking with another adult in the room, or talking with their sibling. Learning to wait your turn—plus developing the social skill of recognizing when it is okay to just butt in—takes time to unfold.

As children mature, they become less impulsive and capable of interrupting less frequently, unless you reinforce and maintain their interrupting behavior.

If your children are getting older and continue to interrupt constantly after your attempts to redirect them and after countless requests that they stop interrupting, you need a new approach. It may be time to ask yourself if there is something else going on that you are not addressing. This something else could be that you accept their interruptions after bedtime, maybe all through the night.

If the co-sleeping habit in your household includes an intrusive element, such as your child calling out or entering your bedroom or bed in the middle of the night, you may be reinforcing your child's daytime interrupting behavior without realizing it.

When you habitually co-sleep with your children in reaction to their intrusions into your room and into your bed, your acceptance of their behavior sends them the message that intruding anytime is okay with you. They figure that if it's okay to interrupt you in your bedroom during your private, adult time, then it's okay to interrupt you by calling you constantly at work, at the dinner table, and any time. Their behavior is consistent, night into day.

If you don't want them to constantly interrupt and demand your attention at their whim during the day, then don't accept this behavior at night.

By co-sleeping in reaction to intrusion, you are rewarding your children for this behavior. So why wouldn't they intrude and interrupt you throughout the day as well?

Simply telling your children to stop interrupting all day long won't achieve your goal. The repetition will just frustrate you and them. Eventually, they will tune you out. Giving your children something to do instead of interrupting when you are busy isn't enough. Your daytime guidance needs to be consistent with your nighttime parenting.

Children will internalize what you do to a far greater extent than what you say. Therefore, the message you will communicate by no longer allowing your children to constantly interrupt your sleep is more powerful than the words you now use to correct interrupting during the day.

Addressing your children's intrusive behavior at night will help your children learn not to constantly interrupt you during the day when you are on the phone, talking with someone else in the room, or in the bathroom.

The behavior that you repeat night after night has a lot of power. If you put your children back to bed when they intrude at night rather than letting them co-sleep, they will learn not to interrupt because you are no longer rewarding the intrusive behavior.

Obviously, if your child is sick or has a legitimate concern, it's okay to wake you up or interrupt you, night or day. But under normal circumstances, you don't have to reward the nighttime intruder.

Keep in mind that if your child is interrupting constantly during the day, this behavior pattern has become a habit in its own right. Once you set bedtime boundaries, you will then be able to effectively help your child limit his or her daytime interrupting habit by using parenting tools that include patience, reminders, and consistency.

Think about These Questions

- Do any of your children interrupt your sleep by calling for you from their rooms night after night? Do you get out of your warm bed? Do you then reward them by going to their room, and then maybe lie down with them until they "let" you leave?
- Do any of your children interrupt your privacy night after night by coming into your bedroom uninvited? Do you reward them for this behavior by letting them sleep with you in your bed?

- Do any of your children come into your bed some time in the night and sleep there without being returned to their own beds?
- Do you react to the interruption by co-sleeping with your children for some of or the remainder of the night? Do you realize that you are rewarding their interrupting behavior?

Respect for Privacy

Both adults and children are entitled to have private time. It is up to you as parents to show your children how to balance being together with having private time by yourselves.

Your Right to Privacy

You have a right to your privacy, even though you are a parent. You have the right to privacy when you go to the bathroom. You have the right to privacy when you change your clothes. You have the right to privacy when you sleep with your spouse or if you want to sleep alone.

Privacy is healthy. It is not the same as secrecy. Secrecy implies deception, hiding something that should not necessarily be kept private. Secrecy is about not letting someone know something that they might be entitled to know.

In addition to your needing privacy for specific reasons, it's also okay to want and to enjoy private, uninterrupted time without your children. That's not to say that you should want to be alone all the time or that you don't enjoy the time you spend with your children. As much as you love your children and their company, you have a right to privacy—not just because you may be doing something that your child shouldn't see—but also because you just feel like having some solitude, some down time with yourself, some thinking time, or quiet adult conversation with your partner. You may feel like reading a book without dividing your attention, or watching a TV show that's enjoyable to you but to no one else in the household. You have the right to sleep privately as well if you want to.

Children Benefit from Privacy

When you break the co-sleeping habit and teach your children to sleep independently, they begin to appreciate their own private time. After they master self-comforting skills and find sleeping and staying in their own beds not so bad, many children enjoy the period of time between getting cozy in bed and falling asleep. It's a time for them to review important parts of the day in their minds, a time to relax without having to perform. It's a time for them to engage in fantasy.

The value of your children's private time in their beds also teaches them how to meet some of their own needs and how to balance alone time with togetherness. Learning this balance is a step along their journey toward becoming securely attached adults.

Less Manipulation

If you feel manipulated by your children into co-sleeping, you probably feel manipulated by them during the day as well. Allowing yourself to be manipulated night and day can make you feel tense and exhausted. It's not good for your children, either. As convincing as they are that they want to be in charge, children are not equipped to make their own child rearing decisions, and they certainly should not be in charge of you.

I often ask families, "Who is in charge?" You might be surprised how often everyone agrees that it is one of the children. Aren't the adults supposed to be in charge?

Do you walk on eggshells trying to avoid your child's objections to your choices? Do you structure your life—during the day and at night—around avoiding a potential tantrum?

Empowerment Without Manipulation

Of course, it's important that children's voices be heard and their feelings and preferences considered. It's okay sometimes to give them that extra cookie or let them stay up a little later when they want to, or go to a restaurant that they like. Children need to feel empowered and be given some leeway.

Parents will tell me about the things their children "make" them do or "won't let" them do. It is often the case that the children who "don't let" their parents spend time together in the family room at night without them or who "make" their parents buy them things are the same children who "don't let" their parents leave after tucking in, and they "make" their parents co-sleep with them. Is this happening in your household? Are your children in charge, night and day?

Your children will feel more empowered by learning how to control their own behavior rather than controlling yours. By giving your children the message that they are in control of the decisions that affect their health and well-being, you are running the risk that they will not feel protected.

As parents, you are adults. Your children probably view you as all-knowing. If they test you, they want you to pass the test and prove that you are the leaders of the family.

The Value of No

Parents who tell others with an embarrassed smile, "I just can't say, 'No' to my child" are viewed by some people as loving, by some as overindulgent, and by others as weak. These parents are ultimately doing their children a disservice. Letting your children be in charge is not the same as empowering them. This type of reactive parenting sets children up to grow into adults who won't be able to say "No" to themselves and who will expect everyone around them to cater to their whims. When this doesn't happen, they'll have trouble coping and will act out, either with anger, pouting, or another inappropriate display.

Children who can't deal with hearing "no" while they are still under your care will not be able to deal with it later. Of course, it's important that your children learn to stand up for themselves, but they also have to learn how to cope. Important life skills—including living with someone else's decision, not getting their way, and being able to adhere to rules—require the development of self-control, self-comfort, and rational thinking.

Children who are brought up by parents who don't say "No" (or who don't mean "No" when they say it) interpret their parents' behavior to mean:

- I can do anything I want.
- My demands should be met all the time.
- Rather than dealing with no, I'll get payoff from making others miserable.
- Fun experiences should have no endings.
- I don't have to do what anyone else wants unless I feel like it.
- I don't have to say no to myself.

Reduced Power Struggles

Your children not listening to you goes hand-in-hand with their perception, and maybe yours, that they are in charge and that they don't have to listen when you say, "No." Your children may be in charge of just you, of both parents, their grandparents, their siblings, or the whole family.

Children who listen to their parents when it's time for bed listen during the day as well. You don't have to engage in the co-sleeping habit as a solution to dealing with your children's screaming, crying, name calling, or unreasonable demands for attention at bedtime. You have a choice. You can learn to expect your children to listen to you. Parents who give in to their children's demands at bedtime often feel helpless and trapped because their children control them by demanding the co-sleeping outright or their children manipulate them and wear them down through crying, having tantrums, begging, hugging, making promises, and other emotional means.

Decreased Whining

Just the word *whining* makes most parents cringe. Whining is a high-pitched, prolonged, self-pitying protest that some children use constantly in response to being told no. If you give in to whining, you will get more whining.

Often, parents will only give in to co-sleeping sometimes. Giving in sometimes is the most powerful form of reinforcement. Like slot machines, they pay off sometimes, and you never know when that will be or how much you need to stay with it. Just when you're about to give up, there it is—the jackpot. For your children, the jackpot is getting what they want, even after you have said no repeatedly. At night, the jackpot for whining is getting you to co-sleep. Is the whining habit part of the co-sleeping habit at your house?

If you give in to whining at night, it's a safe bet that this persistent, annoying behavior works during the day as well. Closely related to whining is begging. "Pleeeease . . . I'll do anything!" Begging is usually done in a whining voice, punctuated with whimpering—and brief pauses to wait and see if you respond. Have you gotten yourself and your child into the co-sleeping habit because your child has begged you to co-sleep and you feel terrible saying no to such desperation? Do you give in to desperate behavior during the day, too?

Many parents in the co-sleeping habit with their children feel manipulated not only at bedtime, but during the morning routine as well. Whining, avoiding getting ready for the day, and having to be prompted every step of the way through a daily morning routine is simply an extension of the bedtime problem.

A variation on whining and begging, and an effective form of manipulation for many children, is the repetition of this sentence: "But I don't feel like it."

Whether your children are two years old or teenagers, if you give in to whining, begging, and "But I don't feel like it" at bedtime, you are ensuring power struggles and frustration all day long. Teaching your children how to sleep without you will give them a sense of security, pride, and self-control that will translate into more cooperative daytime behavior.

It's up to you as parents to guide your children to express their wishes in a less annoying, and more acceptable way. It's up to you to teach them that sometimes we all have to do things we don't feel like doing. That's part of earning the freedom to do what we *do* feel like doing.

Giving in may seem easier, but if you are consistent in your plan to set better bedtime boundaries, you will be working toward solving the manipulation problem. Once your children learn that manipulation, whining, and carrying on don't work, they will find more effective ways to communicate with you, the extended family, their friends, and their teachers.

When you give in to your children's manipulations, they could grow up believing:

- Manipulation is the most effective way to get what I want.
- It's okay to control people.
- I don't have to control myself.
- The more desperately I act, the bigger the payoff.
- I should always get my way.

Smoother Transitions

Life is filled with transitions. Some are developmental, for example, a child leaving the bottle or breast for a cup. Some transitions are planned, for example, moving from the city to the suburbs. Others transitions, such as being alone after your spouse walks out on you, are sudden and not your idea. Most transitions and changes, particularly the ones that take you by surprise, are uncomfortable, and they trigger stress.

One of the earliest transitions encountered by children is a natural one that occurs no matter what—day turns into night, and night turns into day. Adjusting to this reality, coping appropriately with it, and even coming to appreciate it, is not easy for all children. It is up to you to show them how to deal with the transition from daytime to bedtime.

If you overprotect your children from developing their inner resources to cope with this natural nighttime transition, you may find that they won't know how to deal with endings, beginnings, and changes during the day.

If you help your children develop good coping skills, their discomfort and stress about bedtime will diminish as they adapt to this natural transition. Children who use their coping skills at night deal better with transitions and change during the day.

When raising your children, you want to give them messages that help them develop the ability and courage to cope with transitions, change, and stress. You know that one day, they will be on their own, and you won't be with them every minute to do the coping for them.

You want to communicate to your children through your actions at bedtime that:

- Bedtime is not just an ending. It is a natural part of the cycle of the day.

- You will help them deal with the transition, but not do it for them.
- You believe they can learn how to deal with change and new challenges.

Adapting to Transitions

You want your children to feel capable of dealing with transitions that are appropriate to their age. Bedtime can become a normal transition in your household. The key is to teach them how to make this transition, to be supportive, but not to do it for them.

Even before they are toddlers, your children are learning about transitions. Some of the frequent transitions that are built into most babies' lives include:

- Seeing or hearing you enter the room and leave the room.
- Sucking on the nipple, bottle, or pacifier begins and ends.
- Being dropped off at daycare or a babysitter's house and then being picked up later in the day.
- Experiencing weather transitions—sunny to rainy, light to dark.
- Seeing and hearing a visitor enter the home and then later leave.
- Learning to wave bye-bye.

Teaching your toddler how to cope with transitions can easily break down at bedtime. This happens because many parents take on their children's discomfort and stress rather than helping them through it.

It's really obvious when a child is unhappy that day has turned into night, that it's bedtime, and that they don't want to deal with it. They want to continue to play, snack, snuggle, laugh, run around, and do all the things they enjoy during the day. Being with you while they fall asleep and then keeping you with them or going with you to your bed makes daytime never end. Children give clear signals of resistance to making a change that is not their idea. They cry, whine, avoid, scream, beg, plead, thrash around, and sometimes throw stuff.

Rather than seeing their child's reaction as a signal to teach their child self-comfort skills and provide support during this transition, some parents overreact and make the mistake of assuming that making this natural transition is too hard for their child. This is how the reactive co-sleeping begins. Rather than being based on an attachment parenting plan, this type of co-sleeping is based on your fear, guilt, or simply not knowing what to do.

Unfortunately, the message that the child receives when this type of reactive co-sleeping becomes a habit is that transitions, separations, and other changes that take place during the day are "too hard" as well.

Children who are not shown how to transition to bedtime can develop difficulty with other transitions, particularly when the transition is from something they are enjoying to something they don't feel like doing. For example, have you noticed that as much as your child resists going to bed, your child also resists getting out of bed in the morning? Getting up in the morning can be just as tough a transition as getting to sleep at night.

The lack of training in endings and beginnings at bedtime also shows itself in the child who will not turn off the television when asked, who cries when it's time to leave the playground or a friend's house, or who won't cooperate during the morning routine.

When you help your children make a smoother transition to bedtime and help them adjust to the fact that each day ends and then a new day begins, other transitions will be easier for them and you will be less stressed as well.

Your Feelings about Bedtime

Do you feel sorry for your children when they have to end their day and go to bed? Do you view it as a sad or threatening thing? Or do you have the perspective that the transition from day to night is a natural part of a cycle that can be greeted in a happy way?

It's important to examine the meanings you attribute to the day ending for your child. You can be sure that your attitude and emotions will be transmitted to them.

If you have had a difficult time settling down your child at bedtime, your frustration may be showing. Calming yourself down and learning how to cope better yourself with your child's bedtime issues will help your child deal better with the transition from day to night and with the other normal transitions in everyday life.

Part II

How to Break the
Co-Sleeping Habit

If you have read the book up to this point, you understand the benefits of setting bedtime boundaries and breaking the co-sleeping habit. If you are ready to move forward, let this part of the book serve as your guide.

Change will occur only if you make it a priority. In order for you to have success in helping your children change the co-sleeping habit, you must start by dealing with yourself.

First, you will learn how to become a calm, assertive leader in your family. Approaching your children from a position of loving strength is key to your success in supporting them through the process. Chapter 4 will show you how.

Then, you will learn how to overcome the barriers inside your head that have stopped you from breaking the co-sleeping habit before now. Changing your thinking is essential to changing the sleep patterns in your household. Chapter 5 will show you how.

Once you understand more about parental leadership and how to challenge negative thought patterns, you will be ready to set better bedtime boundaries.

Chapters 6, 7, and 8 address different age groups. Chapter 9 applies to children of any age.

For some children, their level of maturation does not match their chronological age. Development can be uneven. For example, you might have a verbal, precocious four-year-old who seems more like an elementary-school-age child, or a thirteen-year-old who functions like a younger child. If you feel that your child's maturity level is on the border between preschool and kindergarten, read both Chapters 6 and 7 and use the information that applies to your child's needs. If your child is on the border between elementary and middle school, read both Chapters 7 and 8 and use the information that applies. You are the best judge of which techniques to choose and apply.

CHAPTER 4

How to Become a Calm, Assertive Leader in Your Home

Think back to the adults you admired the most and who encouraged you the most when you were a child. Maybe it was one of your parents, grandparents, or a beloved aunt or uncle. Or maybe it was someone outside your family, or even someone who touched your life for only a short time—a coach who brought out the best in you, the parent of a friend of yours whom you respected, or a teacher who believed in your ability in spite of your self-doubt.

When you think back, there's almost always someone who believed in you and boosted your confidence—someone who helped you see the magic inside yourself. That person played a leadership role in your life. That person taught you to trust yourself. Use the images and strength from your memory of that person to help you become a parent with leadership qualities.

Just remember that parenting is a form of leadership. If you decide that it is time to encourage and teach your children how to sleep independently because you believe it would be in the best interest of your children and your family, you can learn how to make that change. You can guide your children based on your intimate knowledge of how they think and function. Your decisions as a parent should be intentional, not reactive.

Intentional parents are leaders in the home. They respond to their children's needs rather than react to their children's demands. Intentional parenting is based on your evaluation of how to meet your children's needs and maintain balance within your family.

Leadership Is Based on Trust

Being an effective leader as a parent is not about winning power struggles or dominating your children or using fear tactics. It is about support, guidance, and trust.

It begins with trusting yourself. If you believe in your heart and mind that your motives are valid—and if you trust that your children have the ability to develop their inner resources for coping—then your children will trust you when they face new challenges. Their trust in you as a leader will help them accept your guidance and support as they learn to cope with the discomfort that is a natural part of the process of change. Your trust in yourself and in your children is an essential ingredient in your success in breaking the co-sleeping habit and teaching your children how to sleep independently.

On the other hand, if you don't trust your own motives, if you think that you are basically selfish and mean for putting your children through a process of change that is not their idea, and if on top of that, you think your children are incapable of adapting to a new sleep routine, then your children won't trust you when you attempt to break the co-sleeping habit. Why should they?

If you try to apply specific techniques for breaking the co-sleeping habit within this context of uncertainty, your children's discomfort will build into loud and persistent avoidance, and you will find yourself in a miserable power struggle, not only with them, but with yourself. You'll get confused and retreat—defeated and guilt-ridden. Or, you will yell and insist that they do as you say. Neither one of these reactions is healthy or effective for you or your children. Your position as a parent leader will be undermined by these actions.

Effective leadership in the parenting role is not about forcing your children to do what you want. It's about making parenting decisions that are in their best interest and doing your best to help them feel safe enough to cooperate with you. If you have established a secure bond with them, they will continue to feel secure and bonded as you guide them through the difficult task of growing up. This is true not only when talking about toddlers or elementary-school-age children, but also for preteens and adolescents as trust issues become even more complex.

Consistency to Maintain Your Children's Trust

If you have established a secure, loving bond with your children, then they already trust you. But as your children grow, they will test you to make sure that you continue to be trustworthy.

Testing is normal, and your children want you to pass with flying colors. As your children get older, their methods of testing you will become more elaborate and challenging. Even preteen and teenage children want you to pass.

If you are inconsistent with your children—if they never know when you'll be in a good mood and when you'll be impatient, or if they never know when you'll give in to them and when you'll hold your ground—you will make it harder for them to trust you. Why should they believe it when you tell them they'll be okay? Your child may think:

I'm okay right now, but what about later?
Just because I was okay last night, tonight may be different.

To build and maintain your leadership role with your children, they need to know that they can count on you and your response to them. They need you to be calm and in control in the face of their acting out and limit-pushing behavior. This is not to say that you accept their behavior. The key is to accept them and to expect more of them. Your children need the consistent message that they have the magic inside themselves to cope with bedtime and that you know what is best for them. If you are consistent, you will consistently pass their tests.

Consistency is not the same as being rigid. It's okay to let your children stay up a little later on a special occasion or holiday. The point is that you and your partner are the decision-makers. Rather than reacting to your children's whining, begging, or other manipulative behaviors, you are in charge of deciding when it's okay to bend and be flexible.

Communicate Confidence in Your Children

Your children aren't going to change their bedtime behavior just because you tell them to. You already know what happens at bedtime when you get into a power struggle. Your children will change their bedtime behavior when they sense that you truly have confidence in them that they can do it. If your behavior communicates doubt about their competence to be successful participants in breaking the co-sleeping habit, they will sense right away that your efforts are only on the surface—and that you don't really believe in what you're doing. When it comes to breaking an entrenched habit, surface efforts will fail. As a leader, it is your job to instill confidence in the individuals that look up to you.

Sensing your confidence that they are capable of sleeping without you will increase their self-confidence.

The Value of Modeling Calm and Assertive Behavior

Maintaining your children's trust and supporting their development of self-confidence and coping skills requires that you stay calm, while at the same time, asserting yourself as a parent.

Staying Calm

Yelling, becoming frantic, and making empty threats are not compatible with good leadership. Overreactions may have become a habit in your relationship with your child. Take yourself out of that space. You are the adult. If you want your children to calm down—to stop crying, yelling, name calling—you need to model that behavior. Why should they be able to do something that you don't do yourself?

Your staying calm on the surface is not enough. If you avoid yelling but you are clenching your jaw and your eyes are darting about, they know you are not really calm. You're faking it, and it will be obvious. You need to be calm on the inside. You need to let go of having to win, of being offended, and of taking the bait. These are all reactions that will get you nowhere toward your goal of supporting your child in breaking the co-sleeping habit. Your children take their cues from you. If you are frantic underneath, they will be too.

Assertive Behavior

Being assertive basically means that you are neither passive nor aggressive in your parenting. Passive behavior means doing nothing, giving up easily, or not following through. Aggressive behavior is being nasty or threatening.

Assertive behavior is stating what you want in a calm, clear manner using appropriate language. Assertive behavior is at the heart of the leadership role of parents, and it takes practice. The assertive style of communication is essential for breaking the co-sleeping habit.

Not only are you more likely to get what you want from your children if you are assertive rather than passive or aggressive, you are also modeling the behavior you want them to learn. Modeling assertive behavior when supporting your children in breaking the co-sleeping habit will teach your children to be less helpless (passive), less manipulative (passive-aggressive), and less disrespectful (aggressive) at bedtime.

What Limit Setting Teaches Your Children

Setting limits for your children is not a form of deprivation. Rather, it's the part of parenting that teaches them when to stop. Knowing how far to go is an important life skill. We all have limits imposed by society, laws, ethics, the wishes of others, and eventually our own good sense. If you don't teach your children about limits, how will they know when to let go of an argument with a peer or how to plan for meeting a deadline?

Children feel more secure when they know what their limits are. If you don't teach your children about limits and their value, if there are no limits at your house, or if limits change day to day, the world will remain a scary, unpredictable place for your children.

Limit setting is an important part of your job, not only during the day, but also at night. If you engage in the co-sleeping habit because you feel you can't say "No" to your children, you are sending the message that they are in control of the major decisions in their lives, and that it's okay for them to be in control of you. Your children are not learning good self-regulation skills.

Regaining Your Authority

The word authority is often misunderstood. It doesn't mean being overly strict, unfair, unreasonable, callous, or cold. Rather, having authority means being in charge because you have had more life experience than your children. Even if you feel shaky in your knowledge about parenting, you know more than they do about it. That makes you an authority.

Encouraging Your Partner to Co-Lead with You

If you are a single-parent household, you will make the plan and take action on your own. If there are two parents in the household, you will need to plan and take action together. Making an effective plan and following through as a couple requires that you encourage the other parent (or stepparent) to agree that breaking the co-sleeping habit is a priority that takes commitment and planning and that you will support each other through the process.

Unfortunately, parents often disagree and may argue with each other regarding co-sleeping. One parent may be overinvolved with the child while the other parent feels isolated. Overinvolved parents may not see themselves that way. You might get accused of being unloving when you approach the other parent about your desire to break the co-sleeping habit. If your partner is overly involved with the child, you may feel alone or resentful at night when your partner gives in to, or even encourages, the co-sleeping habit.

Part of your task in the leadership role is to help the other parent see the value in breaking the co-sleeping habit. If you are accused of being unloving, stay calm but focused, rather than getting defensive. Make the effort to understand. Your partner may be confusing the co-sleeping habit with attachment parenting. Your partner may not think your child is ready for independent sleep. Rather than being either passive or confrontational in your style, try to stay calm and supportive, and keep your focus on the goal of working together as coleaders.

Don't make the mistake of underestimating your children. By age three, and even younger, if your children detect that one of you is less wholehearted than the other, or that either of you is hesitant about following through, they will try to sabotage the process. You may have to wait until you have enlisted your partner's complete support to work on breaking the co-sleeping habit. Perhaps you can suggest that your partner read this book, or you can both read it together so that you can be in sync and begin to colead in the process.

For Divorced Parents

If you are divorced, rising above your personal conflicts with your children's other parent so that you can at least try to co-parent about the children's sleeping arrangements is part of your role as a leader. This can be very challenging, but no matter what you think of your ex, your children love and are influenced by their other parent.

You may not be able to convince the other parent to break the co-sleeping habit at his or her house, but you can communicate in a calm, assertive manner why and how you are working on it. Having a co-parenting discussion when you are making a change in your household will let the other parent know that something important is occurring in your children's life. Your children's awareness that you had a discussion will let them know that you are comfortable sharing the information with their other parent even though you are divorced. So even if the other parent doesn't go along with breaking the co-sleeping habit, you will have empowered yourself and your children.

CHAPTER 5

How to Challenge Your Inner Barriers

Have you thought about breaking the co-sleeping habit before now, but your thinking didn't translate into action? What has stopped you in the past?

It's easy to blame your partner, or even worse, your children. What stops most people from breaking any habit, including the co-sleeping habit, are internal barriers, not external barriers. Your own thought processes and insecurities have created the barriers that stopped you from breaking the co-sleeping habit.

Self-Talk

It's not events or other people that create your feelings or your decisions. Rather, it's your own internal processes—your thoughts, beliefs, and interpretation of events—that create your feelings and your decisions. Your own personal thought process is like an ongoing internal monologue. This internal monologue is known as "self-talk."

What you say to yourself, and how you say it, becomes so automatic over the years that you may be unaware that you are "talking" to yourself. Sometimes we tell ourselves things that are exaggerated and not based on evidence. The goal of this chapter is to increase your awareness of your self-talk so that you can change any exaggerations or misconceptions that have created barriers to your breaking the co-sleeping habit.

The distorted or exaggerated self-talk that you have in your head can create barriers that paralyze you from taking new actions. Consider that it may have been your own internal monologue, your own thinking process, that has stopped you so far from taking the new actions that could have improved the sleeping arrangements in your home.

You have a choice. You can continue to paralyze yourself with your self-talk, or you can empower yourself by challenging your internal barriers. You can actually learn how to change the content and style of your own self-talk.

How Your Self-Talk Can Keep You in a Box

You can't change a habit simply by following a list of techniques. If you could, then breaking habits would be simple—like following a recipe. But there's more to it than that.

Think about all the people who go to the doctor with symptoms that include shortness of breath and fatigue. After doing some tests, the doctor tells them that to feel better and live longer they have to change some habits. The list might look something like this: Quit smoking, give up fatty foods, eat more vegetables, and get off the couch and exercise at least thirty minutes every day. Most of these people already knew what they had to do to feel better and to live longer before going to the doctor. They've already tried to break their bad habits and change their lifestyle. But their efforts were half-hearted and they slipped back quickly.

Although some will try again after seeing the doctor, most people fail to follow through with the doctor's recommendations. Why? Don't they want to feel better and live longer? Of course, they do. What prevents them from breaking old habits and establishing a healthier lifestyle is their inner barriers, their self-defeating thought process, which goes something like this:

- I can't change. It's too late.
- I'm surrounded by other people's cookies and candy at the office.
- I'll wait for a more convenient time.
- What if I go through all that pain and I still feel lousy?
- I know people who smoke and live long lives.

They tell themselves they can't do it. They blame other people and circumstances. They give themselves permission to avoid and procrastinate. They let the fear of failure and other fears get in their way. Finally, they rationalize that they'll be fine without making any changes.

With convincing arguments such as these, rehearsed over and over again, why would they stop smoking, change their eating habits, or be less sedentary? They argue very effectively, through their own thinking, or self-talk, to keep things the same because it's easier.

For most people, their thought process has become so automatic that they don't recognize that they are sabotaging their goals with their own thinking. They think external reasons are keeping them from breaking their habits. So they blame circumstances that are outside of their control, like the past (*I come from a long line of smokers; it's in my blood*) or events in the present (*There's candy all around me at the office*) or built-in personal traits that translate into negative labels (*I'm too lazy*).

Change Your Thinking to Break the Co-Sleeping Habit

The truth is that events or circumstances do not keep you in your rut; rather, you keep yourself there by the meaning you place on events and the way you think about yourself. You can't control events—but you do have the power to change the way you look at things and how you view yourself.

Coming to understand that your own thought process has the power to either sabotage your efforts or to empower you is the first step on your journey to breaking any habit, including the co-sleeping habit. No amount of advice is clever enough to break the co-sleeping habit if you don't identify, challenge, and change the self-defeating thought pattern that prevented you from moving forward in the past. Only you can examine and change your own thinking. When you identify that part of your thought process that keeps you from achieving your parenting goals, you can overcome these internal barriers and make positive changes in your family life.

No one is born with thinking habits, but everyone develops them. Self-defeating thought patterns, as well as empowering ones, don't just emerge all of a sudden when you become a parent. Your thinking habits began to develop in childhood and were strongly influenced by how you were raised. In the same way, your children's beliefs about themselves and how to approach situations are influenced by you.

In previous chapters you learned about the messages your children receive through their interactions with you and how you can help them change misconceptions that have created barriers in their adaptation to both their nighttime and daytime lives. In this chapter you will learn to identify and challenge your own thinking barriers, the self-talk inside your own head that has prevented you from breaking the co-sleeping habit.

Your internal barriers, your own self-doubt and misconceptions—not your child's behavior—are what have kept you in the parenting rut of the co-sleeping habit. Once you learn to identify your own thinking barriers you will be able to challenge them and replace them with more confident and positive ways of thinking that will free you to be a calm, assertive leader who is equipped to follow through on an effective plan to break the co-sleeping habit.

Types of internal barriers that you need to overcome include:

- Powerless thinking
- Excuses to procrastinate
- Blaming others and circumstances
- Fear of failing as a parent

These four types of internal barriers can stop you from changing any habit, including the co-sleeping habit. Let's look at them one at a time so that you can identify and eliminate your own internal barriers that might get in your way as you work toward breaking the co-sleeping habit.

How to Overcome Powerless Thinking

Powerless thinking is a habit that can keep you in a box. If you believe that you can't do something, then the chances are that you won't be able to accomplish it. Powerless thinking is the enemy of changing any behavior or habit.

Powerless thinking does not just emerge all of a sudden when you become a parent. It begins early in your life. For example, if you were a ten-year-old who was in the habit of saying out loud or to yourself, "That's too hard. I can't figure it out," you have probably rehearsed this thought pattern over the years and applied it to numerous situations, including changing your reactive parenting style. Many parents have said to me, "Changing the bedtime routine sounds good, but it's just too hard," or, "I can't figure out how to get my son to stay in his own bed."

It's true that changing routines is hard, and teaching your children to do something they have not done before is challenging, but if you tell yourself it's "too hard" or that you "can't do it," you will be powerless, and you and your child will remain in the same box—just where you started.

If you tell yourself that you can't break the co-sleeping habit with your child because you don't have the time, because you are too tired at night to follow through with something new, because your child is too easily upset, because it's too hard or too late, or because of all the other possible reasons that you can think of—then you won't change it. You will be paralyzed.

So what's the alternative? Instead of telling yourself, "I can't do it," or "It's too hard," give yourself a new message. Tell yourself that even though breaking the co-sleeping habit may be difficult or challenging, you can accomplish it with effort and persistence. Tell yourself: "It's not true that I can't. This is just an exaggeration. I have the option of deciding to make breaking the co-sleeping habit a priority. I can learn how to support my children through the process. If I decide I really want to do this for my children, my family, and myself, I can." Notice that the powerless self-talk is an exaggeration and that the replacement self-talk is realistic.

By modifying your self-talk in this way, you will increase your chances for success enormously. Keep in mind that the word "can't" is paralyzing, exaggerated, and usually not true. Be aware that variations on "I can't" that mean the same thing include "I'll never be able to"; "I'm too lazy," "too busy," or too anything else; and "It's impossible." You can send up the red flag and then challenge this extreme language that makes you powerless.

How to Stop Making Excuses to Procrastinate

On the surface, procrastination looks like waiting or putting something off until some future time for a logical reason. But at its heart, procrastination is purely avoidance. It is an excuse to keep things the same. By avoiding the task of breaking a habit with excuses that seem rational and reasonable on the surface, you reduce your anxiety. That may feel good for a little while, but underneath you know you're avoiding the issue and you're still stuck with the co-sleeping habit. So the anxiety returns full throttle later on. The longer you procrastinate, the worse it gets. The most common excuse to procrastinate that I hear from parents is: *This isn't a good time to make a change.*

This statement, which represents the parent's self-talk, is an internal barrier to change that is usually followed by a specific reason, or excuse, explaining why this isn't a good time to make a change.

Excuses parents make to procrastinate include:

- He's too young. I'll wait until he starts kindergarten.
- She's too insecure. I'll wait until she starts first grade.
- I'll wait until winter because it'll be easier when it gets dark earlier.
- I'll wait until summer because we won't have to deal with the school schedule.
- I'll wait until I have more time.

On the surface, waiting seems justified. There's some sort of logic to it. But when the heart of the thinking is really an excuse to procrastinate, then it's not about waiting—it's about avoidance.

Waiting is not necessarily a bad thing—if you have a specific reason and time in mind, like waiting until next weekend or waiting until the next school break. But giving yourself a vague message about waiting is a form of procrastination and avoidance that keeps you and your child in a box.

Notice your excuses to wait. Are they vague? Are they really excuses to procrastinate? How long do you really want to wait to break the co-sleeping habit? Think about how long you have waited already.

The Barriers Created by Blame

It's not other people or circumstances that stop you from changing your behavior. As an adult, you are the decision-maker about your behavior. Once you stop blaming and you begin to own the co-sleeping habit as something you have created, you are on your way to being able to change it.

Blame is easy; taking responsibility is more difficult. The tricky part is that you may believe that other people and events outside yourself really are in control of the sleeping arrangements in your household. If you buy into this, then how can you change anything?

Think about all the things and people you can blame for maintaining the co-sleeping habit. Your self-talk may include lists of circumstances and people who are to blame for your keeping things the same.

Blaming Has Kept Many Parents in the Co-Sleeping Box: What about You?

- Blaming your job
  - *I get home too late to work on changing the sleep routine.*
  - *I'm too tired from work to deal with the co-sleeping problem.*

- Blaming your spouse
  - *My wife is so overinvolved with the kids that I've given up on changing the co-sleeping.*
  - *My husband doesn't support me with raising the kids.*
- Blaming your parents or in-laws
  - *The kids' grandparents sabotage our efforts. They won't stop co-sleeping on weekends.*
  - *My wife's parents are impossible. They guilt-trip my wife into co-sleeping with our toddler.*
- Blaming the school and children's activities
  - *The teachers give too much homework, so my kids are up too late to deal with a change.*
  - *She's learning soccer and shouldn't have a change in bedtime routine right now.*
- Blaming the way you were raised
  - *I'm just like my mom—I can't say no to my kids.*
  - *I don't want my child to feel alone and afraid the way I did growing up.*
- Blaming your children
  - *My eight-year-old son still makes me lie down with him until he falls asleep.*
  - *Our five-year-old daughter is too insecure to sleep through the night by herself.*

How to Stop Blaming and Take Control

Even though your job, your spouse, your parents, your in-laws, the school, your children's activities, the way you were raised, and your children's behavior are all realities, they are all external to you. You have a choice about how to deal with all of it. You can blame any or all of these things for your own behavior, or you can empower yourself with self-talk that moves you forward.

Rather than blaming your job for stopping you from breaking the co-sleeping habit, you can tell yourself that even though you are busy and tired, it's worth the trouble to put thought and energy into a parenting plan that will affirm your leadership as a parent and help your children feel more secure.

Instead of blaming your husband or wife, you can decide to engage your spouse in a productive, loving discussion about how you feel the children and family would benefit from changing the sleep arrangements in your household.

Rather than dwelling on the obstacles that might be put up by your parents or in-laws, you can go ahead with a new plan for nighttime parenting in your own household. The older generation may come around later on. Even if they don't, you can choose to focus on what you can accomplish and not so much on what is outside of your control.

School and other activities take up a significant amount of the family's time and energy. Rather than viewing these essential elements of your child's life as obstacles, take them for what they are—important developmental tasks. Teaching your child how to sleep independently will increase his or her coping skills, and this will have a positive impact on what happens with school, sports, and everything else. Any difficulty or loss of sleep you and your child have during the transition from the co-sleeping habit to independent sleep will be worth it in the long run.

Although the way you were raised influences you—either by making you feel that you should do the same thing or by catapulting you into doing the opposite—you can make the choice to be a parent who meets the needs of your own individual children. Your children are not you, and you are not your parents. Your past is not the barrier to change—it's the stuff you tell yourself about the past. You can challenge your thinking habits. You can say to yourself, for example, "I share some of my mother's traits, but there are many ways that I am a unique person." You can say to yourself, "My children don't necessarily feel the way I did when I was growing up. I am giving a lot more thought to parenting them, and they know how much I care."

One of the biggest blame barriers is blaming your children for the co-sleeping habit. Saying that your children make you lie down with them or your children don't let you change the sleeping arrangement is the same as saying that your children are in charge of their own upbringing.

Even though your children's behavior affects you, it cannot cause your own behavior. When your child cries after being tucked in or clings to you at night, these behaviors are signals that you need to respond to with a well-thought-out plan, not with the guilt and anxiety that have kept you in the co-sleeping habit. Rather than interpreting your child's behavior to mean that you must stay in the co-sleeping habit, you can choose to view your child as looking for reassurance from you that he or she can cope. Your child needs you to be a calm, assertive leader. Your child wants you to pass the test and prove that you know best so that he or she can feel secure—that you will be there to help with important life transitions.

So stop blaming your child's behavior for keeping you in the co-sleeping habit. That behavior may really be telling you that it's time to make a change.

Fear of Failure Impedes Success

Fear of failing at something stops many people from even trying new things. They would rather keep things the same and stay unhappy than put in the effort and then fail. Doing something new just seems like too much of a risk in the face of already too low self-esteem.

Many parents have such a huge and exaggerated fear of being bad parents that they don't change anything. They just keep things the same, even if what they are doing isn't working. It just seems safer to do that. Are you that type of parent? Are you so afraid of making a mistake that you would rather keep the status quo even if it's not working for your children and family? Do you feel guilty about things that might happen, things that you invent?

If you have fear of failing as a parent, you are not alone. It is a very common fear. Much of the self-talk of parents who live in fear of failing their children consists of stuff they just make up to guilt-trip themselves.

Here are some of the things that parents tell themselves might happen if they try to teach their children, toddlers through teens, how to sleep independently:

- My child won't love me any more if I don't stay with her through the night.
- My child will be mad at me if I make him go back into his bed.
- My child will take it as a rejection if we tell him he has to sleep in his own room.
- My bond with my child won't be strong anymore if we sleep in separate beds.
- My child will grow up to be insecure if she has to face sleeping alone.
- If I try to make a change, I'll do everything wrong and mess up as a parent.
- I have already failed as a parent because of the divorce. I have to make up for this by staying with my child through the night.

These types of self-talk statements come from your own fears and insecurities, not from information on child development. They are projections, stuff you invent about the catastrophes that will occur if you implement a plan that makes your child uncomfortable.

It is your job as a parent to help your children through the discomfort of change, not to avoid change. It is your job as a parent to teach your children age-appropriate self-comforting skills so that they can learn to cope, not only with independent sleep but also with all the changes that will occur as they grow.

How to Start Trusting Yourself as a Parent

Parenting based on fear and guilt will simply filter down to your children. They will sense your insecurities and grow up with their own fears of failure.

So what can you do? You can be honest with yourself. Ask yourself if you are avoiding making a parenting plan to break the co-sleeping habit in order to "protect" your children—or to protect yourself from your exaggerated fears of failing as a parent. Take notice of the exaggerations and misconceptions in your thought process concerning your relationship with your children. Notice if you are jumping to conclusions that are based on fear and guilt. Challenge your self-talk.

Then, replace your fear of failure self-talk with calm, more realistic thinking. Instead of catastrophic self-talk, say to yourself something like this:

- If I am sensitive and calm in my approach to breaking the co-sleeping habit, I will not hurt my children by teaching them how to sleep without me.
- My children know I love them even when I ask them to do something they don't want to do, like eat their vegetables or come in from playing.
- Co-sleeping does not make up for the divorce.
- My children need me to guide them in a loving way and teach them how to cope.
- My children's anger in the face of change is not a rejection of me. It just means they need support in learning how to deal with change.
- Bonding is maintained by the quality of our relationship, not by where we sleep.

Remember what Dr. Spock said many generations ago and what Dr. Sears says today: Trust yourself.

Your Internal Barriers: Co-Sleep Quiz 2

You will apply specific techniques for breaking the co-sleeping habit only if you overcome your internal barriers first. Co-Sleep Quiz 2 is designed to help you identify your internal barriers that take the form of self-talk that can block you from changing the co-sleeping habit.

Once you bring your negative self-talk into your awareness and see how your own thought process is keeping you and your child in a co-sleeping rut, you will be empowered to challenge your thinking and move forward in your parenting.

Completing Co-Sleep Quiz 2 will help you identify the four types of internal barriers that have been described in this chapter: powerless thinking, blaming others and circumstances, excuses to procrastinate, and fear of failing as a parent. A good approach to the quiz is to review the parts of the chapter that are relevant to the statements in the quiz. This is not cheating! Reviewing and applying new information are learning tools that will help you acquire the in-depth understanding that will help you make the changes your want to make.

Co-Sleep Quiz 2 contains statements that represent self-talk barriers that many parents have in their heads that prevent them from breaking the co-sleeping habit.

Even if a statement is not exactly your own self-talk, see if your self-talk resembles any of the statements in the quiz.

Right after Co-Sleep Quiz 2, each statement is discussed so that you can apply your knowledge to your own situation. You're not being graded, so take a risk!

Co-Sleep Quiz 2

You have two tasks in this quiz. First, circle the number of each statement that closely matches your own thoughts or self-talk. Then, in the space provided, write down the name of the internal barrier shown by each of the ten statements. You can use abbreviations if you want to:

- PT (Powerless Thinking)
- BL (Blaming)
- PR (Excuses to Procrastinate)
- F (Fear of Failing as a Parent)

_____ 1. I'll never be able to stop the co-sleeping.

_____ 2. My child isn't ready to sleep alone.

_____ 3. My child doesn't let me leave after being tucked in.

_____ 4. I'm so busy during the day, the only time I have with my child is sleep time.

_____ 5. I don't want my child to feel the way I did growing up.

_____ 6. I have to give my child more leeway because of the divorce.

_____ 7. What if stopping the co-sleeping makes my child less bonded to me?

_____ 8. My child will hate me if I force him (or her) to sleep alone.

_____ 9. What if I try to follow everything in this book and I fail?

_____ 10. My wanting my child to sleep without me is selfish.

If you circled any of the numbers next to any of the statements in Co-Sleep Quiz 2, then you are on your way to achieving your goal of breaking the co-sleeping habit and setting better boundaries at nighttime. Your ability to identify your own thinking or self-talk barriers is the first step to challenging and overcoming them.

It's okay if you didn't label the statements the same way as below. The goal of this quiz is to help you think more deeply about your thinking barriers—not to test you.

The discussion of each statement in Co-Sleep Quiz 2 includes suggestions about how to challenge your own thinking so that you can address the co-sleeping habit more effectively.

Number 1

I'll never be able to stop the co-sleeping is an example of powerless thinking (PT). Watch out for the words *never, can't,* and *too hard* in your self-talk. Giving yourself messages with these words will paralyze you from taking action.

WHAT TO DO INSTEAD

If you detect powerless thinking as one of your internal barriers, give yourself a more empowering and accurate message. In the case of the statement in this example, you could tell yourself instead that although breaking the co-sleeping habit may be a new challenge, you have the resources and motivation to succeed. You may find yourself arguing with yourself, back and forth, the old message with the new one. Give the new empowering message a stronger voice.

Number 2

My child isn't ready to sleep alone is an example of making an excuse to procrastinate (PR). Notice the vagueness of the statement. Waiting for someone to be ready can mean putting off a task forever.

WHAT TO DO INSTEAD

Remember that procrastination is not the same as setting a specific time to begin. Procrastination is usually vague and just a way to put something off. You can tell yourself that if you have taken the time and effort to study this book, then you believe that you and your child are ready to break the co-sleeping habit.

Overcome this inner barrier with action. Look at your calendar with your partner and make a plan together. Decide when you will begin the process of changing the sleeping arrangements in your household. Then, stick to your timetable. Make it a priority. As the time draws near and your anxiety mounts, don't trick yourself into procrastinating by making something else more important.

Number 3

My child doesn't let me leave after being tucked in is an example of blaming your child (BL). Variations of this blaming your child self-talk barrier include statements like: *My child makes me lie down with him until he falls asleep. I have to get up and sleep with my child in her bed when she comes to get me in the middle of the night. My child insists on sleeping between us.*

Think about This: If you give your child control over the decision regarding where and when everyone in the household sleeps, do you also let your child decide who should drive the car? Do you let your children watch inappropriate movies because they won't let you change the channel? Do you let your child decide which homework assignment to do and which ones don't matter? Does your child "make you" buy things that are unhealthy or things you cannot afford?

WHAT TO DO INSTEAD

Instead of blaming your child's behavior for your decisions, take the steps described in the previous chapter to become a calm, assertive leader. Remember that as a parent, it is your job to raise your children to cope. It is up to you to support and comfort your children when facing new developmental tasks—not to give in to them out of your fear or their fears when there is nothing to really fear.

Take responsibility for your actions. If you let your children dictate your actions as a parent, you will fail the test they give you every day, the test to see if you are wise enough and strong enough to depend on as they grow up. It is unfair to blame your children for your own lack of assertiveness as a parent.

Number 4

I'm so busy during the day, the only time I have with my child is sleep time is an example of blaming circumstances (BL). Everyone is busy. Life is filled with circumstances that can make it difficult to take care of our children and their needs. But blaming your job, your schedule, your child's schedule, and all the other externals will block you from being an effective parent.

Think about This: Co-sleeping does not compensate for the time you don't spend with your children while they are awake. Maintaining attachment requires awake time that includes things like listening to your children's stories about their day, playing games, reading together, eating a meal together, going to the store, and meeting their friends.

WHAT TO DO INSTEAD

Instead of blaming your schedule and then feeling guilty about not spending time with your children during the day, find a way to spend more time with them during the week and on weekends. Even young children can help you prepare a meal in the early evening. This can be a fun time for both of you. Instead of retreating to your computer in the evening, play a game with your child or read with your child. Make plans to do brief activities with your child, like walk the dog together or go out for ice cream. Children look forward to these special bits of time with their parents.

Number 5

I don't want my child to feel the way I did growing up is an example of blaming the way you were raised (BL). If this is a concern, you have probably done a lot already to ensure that your child feels loved. Be careful, though. Some parents overcompensate for their childhood issues by overprotecting their own children.

WHAT TO DO INSTEAD

Remind yourself that the past is over. Remind yourself that you and your partner are not the same people as your parents and that your child is not you. You are all individuals. Even though the past has an influence, you are not imprisoned by it, unless you imprison yourself with your own exaggerated thinking.

Stop blaming how you were raised on how you parent your child. Trust yourself to be the best parent you can. If you give your child love and reassurance, and teach your child self-comforting skills, your taking steps toward breaking the co-sleeping habit will not make your child feel insecure, lonely, or unloved.

Numbers 6, 7, 8, 9, and 10 are all examples of self-talk that trigger and maintain fear of failing as a parent (F).

There's nothing more paralyzing than the guilt and avoidance you create for yourself through the fearful messages that you rehearse in your mind over and over again. The self-talk that is at the heart of fear of failure as a parent can take on a variety of forms.

Number 6

I have to give my child more leeway because of the divorce is a combination of fear of failing as a parent (F) and blaming the divorce for the co-sleeping habit (BL).

If you tell yourself that because you put your child through a divorce that you are now obligated to stay with your child when he or she protests after being tucked in or that you have to comfort your child through the night, you are misunderstanding your role as a divorced parent.

You cannot compensate for the lack of an intact family, for the pain of divorce, or for your fear of failure as a parent by engaging in the co-sleeping habit.

WHAT TO DO INSTEAD

If you want to succeed as a parent after divorce, spend quality time with your child during the waking hours, maintain structure and boundaries, teach your child coping skills, and be a reliable, loving role model. You can tell yourself that being divorced gives you more time to spend alone with your child and get to know your child as an individual. You can tell yourself that you will be the best parent you can by having a high-quality co-parenting relationship with the child's other parent.

Number 7

What if stopping the co-sleeping makes my child less bonded to me? is a form of fear of failure (F) sometimes referred to as "catastrophizing."

Catastrophizing is a thought process in which you worry that something terrible will happen if you take a certain action. This type of thinking, derived from fear, will paralyze you as a parent.

WHAT TO DO INSTEAD

Tell yourself that trying a new approach to child rearing is not dangerous. Your bond will not be broken. In the case of parent-child attachment, it is not co-sleeping that maintains the emotional bond as your children leave infancy. It is the quality of the parent-child relationship.

This doesn't mean that you can't continue to co-sleep if this arrangement is based on a parenting plan. But you do not have to be physically available throughout the night for the bond to remain strong. Touching in the form of hugging and cuddling will still be in your relationship.

Number 8

My child will hate me if I force him (or her) to sleep alone is an example of fear of failure (F) that confuses "Hate" with "Anger."

Be careful not to confuse hate and anger. Just because someone you love is angry with you, this does not mean that the person hates you. Children can say hateful things to you when they are angry, but they continue to love you.

Your child might be angry with you when you work toward breaking the co-sleeping habit. This won't be the last time your child will be angry with you. Your child may be angry with you when you turn off the television or when you won't buy an inappropriate video game or a piece of candy or when you say "no" when he or she wants to borrow your car. Does this mean that you should avoid acting like a parent? Of course not.

WHAT TO DO INSTEAD

Keep in mind that anger is a normal, legitimate emotion, like happiness, sadness, or excitement. Your child has the right to express anger. Remind yourself that it is your job to acknowledge this emotion as legitimate and help your child express anger appropriately, without aggression or the violation of someone else's rights.

Also keep in mind that children feel comfortable expressing anger toward a parent whom they trust not to abandon them. It's a compliment to you as a parent when your child is comfortable expressing a wide range of emotions in your relationship.

Number 9

What if I try to follow everything in this book and I fail? is an example of generalizing lack of success on a task to being a failure as a person (F).

First, if you have absorbed the true nature of the co-sleeping habit and then you follow the guidance in this book to change the sleeping arrangements in your household, it is unlikely you will fail. But even if you are not as successful at it as you had hoped, you can examine your actions and see where you need to improve.

WHAT TO DO INSTEAD

Tell yourself that generalizing from failing to change something to seeing yourself as a failure as a parent or as a human being is an unfair leap. Remind yourself that if you generalize from mistakes or inactions to judging your essence as a human being, you will take away your power to succeed in the future.

Number 10

My wanting my child to sleep without me is selfish is an example of fear of failure (F) based on stuff you just made up to guilt-trip yourself.

If you tell yourself that wanting your child to sleep without you is selfish, you probably tell yourself that you're selfish and make yourself feel guilty about a lot of other things.

WHAT TO DO INSTEAD

Review the information in this book that discusses how to raise children who can cope, how the co-sleeping habit can trigger fearful behavior patterns in children as they develop, and how the co-sleeping habit can be a burden for children. See if you can create a competing message and engage in new self-talk that says: *My wanting to keep my child entrenched in the co-sleeping habit may be selfish. I want to help my child cope with sleeping through the night without me for my child's sake.*

CHAPTER 6

How to Set Limits with Your Toddler and Preschooler

If you have read the book up to this point, you are ready to break the co-sleeping habit with your toddler and preschooler. They will be ready if you are ready—even if they don't act like it at first.

You know from reading this book so far that your role as a parent is more complex now than it was when your children were infants. As toddlers and preschoolers, they still rely on you, of course, but in a different way. Now you need you to figure out how to balance comforting them with helping them develop their coping skills so that they don't remain clinging, helpless, and fearful infants as they grow into older children, adolescents, and adults. This balancing act is challenging for parents, particularly when it comes to nighttime parenting.

This chapter is designed to guide you, step-by-step, through the process of breaking the co-sleeping habit and teaching your children how to sleep independently. The plan presented in this chapter is applicable across the many different flavors of the co-sleeping habit. Whether you have been a reactive parent from the start or if you had a plan to co-sleep but have changed your mind (but your child has not changed his or her mind), you will reach your goal if you follow the plan correctly.

Remember to have confidence in yourself and in your child that you can successfully break the co-sleeping habit in spite of the anxiety that the change in the sleeping arrangement might trigger. Changing any habit is uncomfortable for many people at first. But once accomplished, what used to be uncomfortable becomes normal, thus increasing your child's comfort zone as well as your own.

Most children experience and display separation anxiety from approximately the age of one year through eighteen months. After that, they are beginning to develop more effective self-comforting skills that help them cope more effectively with separation from you. However, it is not unusual for separation anxiety to resurface again. Toddlers and preschoolers are susceptible to bouts of separation anxiety when they feel threatened by new situations and life transitions.

You might have noticed your child reluctant to separate from you in the face of new challenges, such as having to deal with sharing you after the birth of a sibling or starting preschool. Sleeping without you after being in the co-sleeping habit with you can trigger separation anxiety in your young child.

It is not necessary or helpful to be alarmed by your child's anxiety. Don't let your child's fears about separation at bedtime trigger your own fears about separating at bedtime. If you over-react, your child's discomfort and fears may be prolonged.

As you move through the steps toward breaking the co-sleeping habit with your toddler or preschooler, you will be shown how to be sensitive to your child's separation anxiety without prolonging it.

To overcome the anxiety associated with change and separation, what your child needs the most is your nurturance and your reassurance that everything will be okay. Encouraging them to use their own emerging skills plus calm, convincing words from you that they are safe, will move your toddler or preschooler smoothly away from the discomfort of separation anxiety at bedtime.

Set the Date

The first step in your action plan to break the co-sleeping habit with your toddler or preschooler is to look at your calendar with your partner and set the date.

Select a date that begins a three- or four-day time period during which you and your child can afford to miss a little sleep, such as a long weekend or a time you can take off from work.

See if you can create this time period rather than putting off your starting date indefinitely. Remember that breaking the co-sleeping habit has to be a priority in order for you to be successful in your goal of teaching your child to sleep independently.

Make sure there is nothing major going on in your family or in your child's life—such as the birth of a baby, your changing jobs, or your child's first day of school after vacation—during the time period you select.

Then, mark it on your calendar and day minder, as you would an important appointment.

If you plan and mark the starting date, you decrease the chance that you will procrastinate. Breaking the co-sleeping habit needs to be a priority or it won't happen.

Prepare Your Child's Space

Now that you have a deadline for breaking the co-sleeping habit with your child, you are ready to prepare your child's personal space. This may be your child's own room, a room your child shares with another child, or some other space that you designate as your child's space. For convenience, let's assume it is your child's own room.

Make sure that the sleeping space is comfortable and appealing. Some children sleep in a crib until age two years, some until age three. Some children transition from their crib to a toddler bed with rails on the side and others go right from the crib into a regular bed. You and your partner can make the decision about the appropriate sleep space for your child.

Make sure the room is uncluttered. Get bins or provide other storage for toys, books, stuffed animals, clothes, and accessories. You could decorate with a few framed photographs or posters that have special meaning for your child. Make your young child's space special and ready for him or her to claim it.

Create Positive Associations for Your Child

You want to create positive associations for your child with his or her personal space before expecting your child to sleep alone in that space. This process should begin in the days before you change the sleep arrangements in your household.

Now that your child's room is ready, begin to use your child's space for play and for prep, meaning changing clothes, brushing hair, and other personal activities that might have taken place in your room or another room before now.

Spend time playing with your child in the space you have created. Play sessions of fifteen to twenty minutes in length a few times a day for several days before the new sleep arrangement begins should be sufficient. Make some of the play active and some of the play more of a quiet time. Read to your child a few times over the days before you start the new sleep arrangement.

Do not lie down with your child in the bed in your child's room at any time. Doing so will work against your goal of encouraging independent sleep.

Spending more time with your child in his or her own room (or the part of the room that you have designated as your child's space) and doing everyday things there will create positive associations, making the room a familiar, happy place in your child's mind when you begin the new sleeping arrangement.

Anticipate That Your Child Will Protest Anyway

Children are resistant to change. Changing a habit that feels good is even more difficult. Even if you do everything right by creating positive associations for your child during the day, it is likely your child will put up a fight about sleeping independently. Sleeping with you feels good. Sleeping alone will also feel good eventually, but the transition will be uncomfortable.

By taking the steps toward independent sleep, you are asking your child to go outside his or her comfort zone and change a habit. This isn't easy for you or your child. But you have decided it's important.

Expect and be prepared for resistance when your child realizes that the co-sleeping is about to end, even if you do everything right. Although by age two, and certainly by three or four, children can make their needs known by talking, they often resort to crying, yelling, or stomping around when upset. Protest surrounding sleep is even more common among toddlers and preschoolers who usually get their way during the day. Anticipate that your young child's reaction to your attempts to change the sleep arrangement may be out of proportion to the situation. Prepare yourself mentally and emotionally for breaking the co-sleeping habit as discussed in Chapter 4 on becoming a calm, assertive leader and in Chapter 5 on overcoming your inner barriers to change.

Plan for and Use Adult Support

It is of great value to realize in advance of changing your night-time parenting that your child will tug at your heartstrings and that it will be hard for you not to react by co-sleeping. In addition to the tools provided in Chapters 4 and 5 to bolster you for the moment of truth, you will also need the support of an adult whom you trust to help you through the first night or two. Before you introduce the new sleep arrangement to your child, make a clear plan to receive support.

If your spouse or partner is involved, then you can plan to support and encourage each other through the process.

If you are alone, let a good friend or family member know what you are planning and why it is in your child's best interest. Ask that person to spend that first and second night with you so that you feel supported in the process. If this is not possible, perhaps a friend or family member would be willing to be available by phone those first two nights so that when you are tempted to give up or need encouragement, you have someone to cheer you on.

Do not hesitate to ask for the support that you set up for yourself on that first night. Even if it is very late, in fact especially if it is very late, and you are tired, your child is protesting, and you are doubting your decision to follow through—that's when you need the support the most.

Your willingness to reach out for support that first night could make the difference between succeeding or failing to follow through with your plan to break the co-sleeping habit.

Plan and Implement an Effective Bedtime Routine

Now that you have prepared yourself and created positive associations for your toddler or preschooler, you are ready to plan and implement an effective bedtime routine.

An effective bedtime routine is not just about changing clothes and hygiene, although these are important. It is also a consistent structure that leads naturally to independent sleep.

It should be a relaxing, calming time that signals the end of the busy day. It clarifies for the very young child the transition from day to night, from high energy to quiet time to sleep. It helps regulate your child.

If you just let your toddler or preschooler fall asleep in day-time clothes on the couch while the TV is on or in the car seat on the way home late at night and then undress their limp bodies and throw them into your bed, this is not a bedtime routine. This is chaos.

A bedtime routine is a logically structured sequence of activities that culminates in your child getting into bed and staying in bed for the night. You don't have to be rigid, but the basic structure should be there, particularly at the start of your new sleeping plan.

It's good if your child is sleepy at bedtime, but not asleep. Engage your child's active participation in the tasks of the bedtime routine. Follow the routine that you have planned, and don't ask for or accept suggestions from your child. Toddlers and preschoolers are not competent to decide on an appropriate time to go to bed or a bedtime routine.

First, Set the Bedtime

If you need information on the amount of sleep your child needs as a toddler or preschooler, consult your child's pediatrician. Decide what time your child needs to wake up in the morning, and work backward from there to set the bedtime. Also consider setting the bedtime early enough so that you have time for yourself afterward.

The length of the bedtime routine depends on the activities you want your child to do. On the nights you bathe your child before bed, the bedtime routine will be longer than the nights when just hands and face get washed. Time for the bedtime routine can vary from fifteen to a maximum of sixty minutes. So be aware of the length of the routine and allow enough time to be done by bedtime.

If your child is three or four years old, you can engage your child in drawing pictures of the tasks in the bedtime routine the next day, after the first night that you implement the new routine. This type of activity can help your preschooler remember the tasks and feel more a part of the process beginning the second night and thereafter. Do not do this during the first night of the new routine. This first night, you need to be a calm, assertive leader who guides your child through the new routine.

Begin the Bedtime Routine in Your Child's Room

Make sure you start the bedtime routine at the time you had set based on the number of hours your child needs to sleep. Changing into pajamas (or robe for a bath) should take place in the same room in which your child is expected to sleep independently. You have already helped your child make positive associations with his or her bedroom during the past few days of play and prep.

If your child has been in the habit of changing clothes in your room or the family room and asks the reason for the change, state gently and without hesitation that, "This is your bedroom and this is where you will be changing your clothes now." If you are questioned further, you can add, "This was Mommy's (or Daddy's or Mommy and Daddy's) decision because you are a big boy (or big girl) now." If questioned further, ignore the questions and move on with the routine. Do not get annoyed.

Escort your child to the bathroom for washing hands and face, brushing teeth, and toileting. Bathe your child if this is a night for a bath before bed. Taking a bath can relax your child and is a good bedtime routine activity. If your child is in diapers, change the diaper in your child's room.

Before escorting your child to bed, make sure all toileting is done, that your child has water near the bed, and that all stuffed animals or other soft objects that will be used for self-comforting are in the bed (or crib). Once all possible needs that involve leaving the bed are met, you are ready to tuck your child in.

Your child should be tucked in and should then fall asleep in his or her bed—not somewhere else and then be placed in bed later. If you place your sleeping child in bed from another location, your child's expectations of where he or she is when partially awake during the night has been violated. Your child will wake up fully and cry rather than go back to full sleep from partial sleep. Why? Because the associations established for falling asleep should stay the same throughout the night. If your child fell asleep clutching Mr. Bear in his bed, then he should be able to reach for and clutch Mr. Bear in his bed during the partial awakenings that occur throughout the night.

Teach Your Child How to Self-Comfort at Bedtime

Bringing out your young children's inner resources and teaching them how to self-comfort without you during the night involves setting limits with yourself by controlling your own desire to do everything for your child. To sleep without you, your child will need to learn how to self-comfort when you are not in the bed. It's your job as a parent to teach your child how to self-comfort by providing tasks and objects that are age appropriate.

Instead of providing 100 percent of the comfort, as during infancy, you are now going to let go a little bit and teach your growing child to learn to provide some self-comfort. This is a healthy developmental task.

If you continue to provide 100 percent of the comforting, you will leave no room for your toddler and preschooler to develop the tools to sleep without you. Have confidence in your young children. Look beyond your toddler and preschooler's babylike exteriors and realize that they are thinking beings with inner resources.

Self-Comforting Objects for Your Toddler or Preschooler

Provide self-comforting objects to help your child fall asleep and stay asleep without you. A favorite stuffed animal or other soft object, a nightlight, or a sippy cup with water can provide comfort.

Self-Comforting Tasks for Your Toddler or Preschooler

At bedtime, give your child self-comforting tasks to do while they fall asleep to help them cope.

For example, say to your child

- "Tell yourself that Mommy or Daddy is nearby."
- "Singing to yourself might help you feel better."
- "Cuddling your stuffed animal (or little blanket) will help you feel better."
- "Close your eyes and think about the pretty flowers we saw today"—or any other calming visual image.

If your child still takes naps, the best time to teach your toddler or preschooler self-comforting skills is at naptime. Naptime can be a dress rehearsal for breaking the co-sleeping habit at night.

Sticker System for Comforting Your Preschooler

For older preschoolers, age four and up, using a sticker system can provide comfort. You could have a chart with the days of the week. Have your child place a sticker next to the days that he or she has successfully fallen asleep and stayed in his or her own bed through the night. The more stickers the child earns each week, the bigger the prize. The prizes don't have to be expensive. They can take the form of privileges.

Keep in Mind Three Key Factors about Prizes

- They have to be important to your child or your child won't work for them.
- They should not be awarded unless they were earned.
- Getting to sleep with you on any basis should not be one of the prizes.

Setting up the sticker system and reminding your child about it at bedtime can provide motivation and comfort to your child.

Balance Comforting with Limit Setting

It should take no more than fifteen to twenty minutes to tuck in your child. During this time, talk with your child or read a story. Sit at the edge of the bed or on a chair next to the bed while your child is in the bed under the covers.

Tell your child, "I'll read you a story, we'll talk for a few minutes, and then it will be time for you to rest up for tomorrow." A more verbal child may ask you why you are doing things differently. Keep your explanation short, simple, and loving. If your child has been in the co-sleeping habit with you in your bed and asks about the new location, simply say in a warm, confident tone, "It's time to sleep in your own bed now. I will help you. You'll be okay."

If you are overly attentive at bedtime and you don't set limits—for example, you lie down regularly with your child who then "won't let" you leave—you are maintaining, rather than breaking, the co-sleeping habit. If you don't set limits through your behavior, you will prevent your child from learning how to sleep without you.

Remember that tucking in has a beginning, a middle, and an end. It might help you to read the story in Chapter 10 about a mother and her four-year-old in which tucking in never ended.

It is up to you as a parent to keep to the boundaries of tucking in so that your child learns about endings. When you tuck in your toddler or preschooler, make sure you do the following:

- Keep the tucking-in process structured and time limited.
  - You can read a story or talk with your child.
  - Tell your child, "I'll read you a story, we'll talk for a few minutes, and then it will be time for you to rest up for tomorrow."
  - As you read or talk, sit on the edge of the bed or on a chair near your child's bed while your child is under the covers.
  - Your partner can be with you the whole time or come in toward the end.
- Make sure your child has everything he or she needs—before he or she is in the bed.
  - All toileting should be done before the child is under the covers.
  - Water should be provided and available next to the bed.
  - Comforting objects, for example, a beloved stuffed animal; a small, soft blanket; a nightlight should be in place.
- Encourage self-comfort.
  - Tell your child that holding the stuffed animal will help him or her feel better.
  - Tell your child to remind himself or herself that you will be in the house.
  - Give your child a pleasant image to focus on.
  - Remind your preschooler about the sticker he or she can earn if you use a sticker system.

- Deal with your child's protests in a calm, assertive manner.
  - Give a reassuring smile as you talk with your child.
  - Do not express your own anxiety.
  - Reassure you child you will be available, but be clear that it is up to them to get their rest.

Disengage

This has probably been the point at which the process of breaking the co-sleeping habit has fallen apart in the past. Read this section carefully on how to disengage successfully.

Disengagement is the signal that tucking in has ended. It sets the limit. It is the hardest part of tucking in for you and your child if you have been entrenched in the co-sleeping habit. Disengagement is the part of tucking in you have not achieved before. But you can achieve it now.

How to Disengage

- Make sure the self-comforting tools are in place.
- Get and give your last hug and kiss.
- Turn out the light and say, "Goodnight."
- Leave the room.

If your child acts upset as you are leaving the room, now is the time to say one or more of the following types of comforting statements. You also want your behavior to communicate these ideas:

- "I will protect you even when I'm not in your room."
- "I will (or the other parent will) be in the house."
- "It's important that you have your own sleeping place and that I have mine."

- "If you hug your teddy bear (or doll or blanket) you can help yourself feel better."
- "You'll be okay. I'll see you in the morning."
- If your child talks about being afraid of monsters, simply say: "There's no such thing as monsters. You're okay."

Once you've made your statements, leave the room even if your child is upset. You will be checking in on your child. Remind yourself that you have been a loving, supportive parent tonight. Here's the evidence:

- You have prepared your child.
- You have made your child physically comfortable.
- You have provided reassurance.
- You have tucked your child in.
- You have provided self-comforting tools.

No matter what your child says or does when you begin to disengage, do not be conned into "one more story," or one more drink or snack, and most importantly, do not linger or become engaged in further conversation.

Your child's difficulty with the idea of sleeping without you means that he or she really needs your help to disengage. Your giving in at this point would not only be a setback, but you would also be prolonging your child's upset in the long run.

How to Deal with Crying

This is where it has fallen apart in the past. This is the part you dread. Your child cries when you leave the room after tucking in.

Give Yourself Comfort and Encouragement

If your child cries when you leave the room after tucking in, the first thing you need to do is to comfort yourself. To help yourself leave your child's room and stay out, dispute the negative thoughts in your head that make you feel guilty.

When you hear yourself think: *I'm making my child suffer*, comfort yourself by telling yourself:

- My child will suffer more in the long run if I continue to enable this dependency.
- I am helping my child through a normal transition.
- I am a responsible, loving parent.
- My child knows I am here.

Reach Out for the Support You Planned

In addition to giving yourself comforting and rational self-talk, look for support and encouragement from your partner or the friend you have chosen to help you during the first few nights.

Don't Blame Your Child for Your Actions

This is also the point as which parents tell themselves, "My child won't let me leave the room." Remember from the previous chapter: stop blaming your child for your behavior. Your child doesn't want you to leave the room because you and your child have been caught up in a habit. But you are changing the habit. After tucking in, reassuring, and providing self-comforting tools for your child as described above, you need to give him or her space and time to internalize what you have said and to practice using the self-comforting tools.

Check In with Your Child

You do not need to let your child just cry it out. Remember that although you have provided tasks and tools for self-comfort, your child does not yet know how to use them. This will come. But as your child is learning how to cope with the tools you have provided, you will be checking in with your child every few minutes to provide reassurance—without touching. The absence of touching is important because if you touch after tucking in, your child will look for your touch throughout the night during partial awakenings, rather than learn to use self-comforting tools. Also, your touching without staying is a tease that can set off more intense crying when you leave the room again after checking in. In other words, touching at this point may comfort you and quiet your child for the moment, but it will make it harder on your child as the night progresses.

Keep the Checking In Brief

Seeing you for twenty to thirty seconds, without your having to say or do anything, is reassuring. You are making the statement by checking in that you are there, in the house, that you are keeping your child safe. You are developing your child's ability to be comforted by a distal stimulus (seeing you) without needing a proximal stimulus (touching) for comfort as your child learns how to self-comfort.

You may spend an hour or more proving that you are really available. But if you are consistent and follow the plan, your child will eventually fall asleep.

How to Deal with Begging and Anger

The best way to deal with begging, bargaining, anger, and other forms of manipulative verbal behavior is to ignore it. If you become engaged in interaction with your child when your child behaves this way, you will either give in, lose your temper, cry, or do something else that makes you fail the test—your child's test to see if you really are a calm, assertive leader who knows what is best and who is equipped to keep your child safe.

If your child expresses anger, the anger is really discomfort about change. As your child learns to use self-comforting techniques, the anger will evaporate. Your child still loves you even when saying, "I hate you."

You can make one or two reassuring statements but do not change the plan. Do not bargain. This isn't the time to be flexible because if you are, you will end up back where you started—in the co-sleeping habit.

What to Do If Your Child Leaves His Bed to Find You

Do not go to bed until your child is asleep. Stay in a nearby room—not your bedroom. If your child comes out to find you, escort your child back to bed. The first time it happens, say, "It's bedtime." After that, no matter how many times your child comes out, whether it is to your bedroom or another room, escort him or her back without interaction, cuddling, or rewards of any kind. Your voice is a reward. Don't use it.

If you provide affection, snacks, water, or anything else reinforcing, the behavior will continue night after night. Do not give in to any demands.

Escort your child back to bed matter-of-factly with no reinforcement for as many times as it takes. This consistent, nonrewarding action on your part is key to learning to fall asleep and stay asleep without co-sleeping.

Your child may pop out of bed five times, ten times, twenty times, thirty times, or more. You may need the emotional support of your partner or friend to win this power struggle.

If at any point you reinforce the popping out of bed behavior with something your child wants, you are conditioning him or her to pop out the number of times it took to get that reinforcement. Even though you may feel like it will never happen, your child will eventually stay in bed and fall asleep.

Enjoy Your Child Sleeping Peacefully and Independently

It might take an hour. It might take two or three hours. But if you have followed the plan correctly, your child should fall asleep. Look at your sleeping child from the doorsill. Savor the image. You and your child have achieved a milestone. Your child is sleeping peacefully without you in the bed. Your child knows that you are in the house providing safety. Your child is at the threshold of making the world a safe place for himself or herself. Give yourself positive messages about what you have accomplished.

Go to Bed and Stop Worrying

When your child is asleep, it is time for you to go to bed and stop worrying. You and your child have made it through the first big hurdle. Rather than react with co-sleeping, you responded to your child's bigger need to learn an important life skill, falling asleep without you.

Even if he or she cried, fussed, yelled, begged, bargained, or expressed anger, your child will always still love you in the morning and will still be bonded to you. Get the rest that you need because there is more work to be accomplished over the next few days.

How to Deal with the Little Intruder

Let's say that you've done everything right. You have set a bedtime. You left adequate time for the bedtime routine and you tucked in your child. You communicated messages of safety and security. You taught your child self-comforting skills at naptime and reinforced them at bedtime. You provided reassurance but didn't linger. And your child finally fell asleep in his or her own bed without you. But—some time after that, maybe an hour later, maybe two, three, or four hours later, there is your little darling, either standing right next to your bed or actually crawling into your bed. What should you do now?

First of all, be alert to it. This is no time to get into the mode of not realizing your child entered your room or your bed.

Then, simply do what you did when your child went to look for you right after being tucked in. The first time, say, "It's way past your bedtime," as your only comment on the way back to his or her bed. Once there, say, "Stay in your bed." There should be no other conversation, no other interaction, no drinks of water, no hugs. The second time, say nothing and escort your child back to bed with no reinforcement of the intrusive behavior of any kind—no conversation, no drinks of water, no hugs. Do this as many times as it takes.

Yes, you're tired. But this effort up front will pay off. Your child will learn not only to fall asleep without you, but also to stay asleep without you. Sleeping through the whole night will provide your child (and you) restorative sleep that is necessary for optimal functioning and good health. If you give in and let your child stay with you in your bed, you'll be back to square one. After all the planning, effort, and progress you have made so far in breaking the co-sleeping habit, it's worth it to go the distance.

Reinforce and Maintain Gains

In the morning, wake your child up at the usual time. Upon wakening, lavish your child with praise for sleeping alone like a big boy or girl. Your approval is a powerful reward for your child. If you are using a sticker system, this is also the time to place a sticker on the day that your child slept without you the night before. Even if your first night was an ordeal, if you were successful in following through and your child eventually slept without you, the sticker was earned (by both of you). Make sure you give yourself some praise as well with positive self-talk about yourself as a parent who is now a calm, assertive leader.

Tonight, repeat the same procedures from the first night. Repeat them night after night. It might take a few nights or a full week before the new bedtime routine takes hold without a fuss from your child.

Over the next few nights, your child will begin to form new sleep associations at bedtime. Instead of associating falling asleep with having you available to touch, your child will associate falling asleep with holding a cherished stuffed animal or a soft blanket or seeing a soothing nightlight. When your child partially wakes during the night, as we all do, your child will be able to fall back into a sound sleep, rather than wake up fully, because the same conditions that were present when originally falling asleep will be available throughout the night. Your child will rely on you less—and rely on himself or herself more—for falling asleep and staying asleep over the next few nights.

Your child may continue to test you from time to time. You will pass the test and make your child feel secure if you continue to provide the same structure, reassurance, and self-comforting tools. The co-sleeping habit will be broken and the new bedtime routine followed by independent sleep will take hold.

CHAPTER 7

How to Teach Your Elementary School Child to Sleep Without You

This chapter will guide you step-by-step to break the co-sleeping habit with your child who is between age five and ten years old. In some ways, your task is more difficult than with a toddler or preschooler, and in some ways, it is easier. It is more difficult because you have been entrenched in the co-sleeping habit for a longer period of time. It is easier because your child is more verbal and has stronger reasoning skills than a younger child.

The plan presented in this chapter is applicable across the many different challenges of the co-sleeping habit. Whether the problem has been tucking in that never ends, being summoned in the middle of the night, your child starting off in your bed but never leaving, your child sneaking into your room or bed, or if you had a plan to co-sleep and have changed your mind but your child has not, you will reach your goal to break the co-sleeping habit if you follow the new plan correctly.

Change is difficult for anyone. But if you are motivated; if you understand the principles of calm, assertive leadership; and if you work on overcoming your inner barriers, you can follow the plan and achieve your goal. Have confidence in yourself and in your child that you can make positive changes together.

In your favor is the fact that, underneath, your children want to be more independent. Elementary school is a time for exploration and the development of meaningful peer relationships. Even if your child acts helpless or clingy, children this age want to be able to cope when you are not right there next to them so that they can stay at a friend's house, be dropped off at birthday party, or go on a field trip with the Boy Scouts or Girl Scouts. They want to overcome their separation anxiety because they want to enjoy themselves more and not feel like a baby. But they can't accomplish this developmental task without your help. They need you to help them move outside their limited comfort zones. Teaching them how to sleep independently will increase their confidence in all their important daytime pursuits.

Before dealing directly with your children to make the actual changes, you need to get ready by making a specific plan that meets the needs of the children and the adults who sleep in the household. Creating your plan for breaking the co-sleeping habit takes place behind the scenes, either on your own or with your partner, and without the involvement of your child. Making a specific plan is critical to the success of the outcome.

Once you have your plan, you are ready to prepare your child. After you prepare your child for what to expect, you will be ready to put your plan into action.

Planning: Set the Date and Get Your Child's Space Ready

See pages 99–100 in the previous chapter on how to set the date and get your child's space ready. Additionally, if your child has not slept in or really used his or her room in so long that it has become a storage area with stuff piled up on top of the bed, be sure to get rid of the clutter.

If there is already a bed in the room, clear it off. You can wait to get fresh sheets and bedding until the day you set your plan into action so that your child can help select the bedding. Or you can freshen up the bed on your own.

Structure the New Bedtime Routine in Advance

The heart of your plan is creating an effective bedtime routine for your elementary school child. An effective bedtime routine is structured. It is a specific series of events that begins at a predetermined time and ends at a predetermined time. Bedtime routines make for good sleep hygiene for anyone, child or adult.

The type of routine that is optimal varies with the age and needs of your child. The key to an effective bedtime routine for children ages five through ten is the provision of explicit structure, repetition, and ritual. These ingredients will meet your child's developmental needs.

You may have noticed that your child creates rules and rituals in symbolic play activities and with friends. Your child might enjoy, or even insist on, watching the same movies over and over again, or asks you to tell the same joke over and over again. Elementary-school-age children love repetition. It makes them feel safe and secure. An effective bedtime routine for your five- to ten-year-old child has three distinct parts:

- Wind-down time
- Prebedtime prep
- Bedtime

Wind-Down Time

An effective bedtime routine in elementary school needs to begin with a calm transition from the busy activities of the day.

119

This part of the bedtime routine is called wind-down time. It comes well before bedtime.

Wind-down time is the beginning of the transition from day to sleep time. It is still part of the child's day, but it is a calm, low-key period of time that includes no physical sports, no homework, and no stress.

Allow sixty minutes for winding down. Why so long? Your child needs to ease into letting go of the day. Typically, children between ages five and ten have an enormous amount of physical as well as mental energy. They need outlets for that energy during the day and then sufficient time to calm down in the evening so that bedtime is part of the natural flow rather than a sudden event that is announced in the midst of intense activity. This means that you will need to wind down too.

This is a time, toward the end of the day, to help your child feel safe, secure, loved, and relaxed. Spend time with your child during this hour, either playing a quiet game, watching TV, reading, or talking. If you plan to watch TV with your child during wind-down time, make sure the show is not overly stimulating. All homework should be completed before wind-down time. A light snack is okay.

This is a time when you and your child can spend some time cuddling if you like. Physical closeness and affection during wind-down time will take the place of sharing a bed during the night.

It should be a relaxing and rewarding time for you as well. Wind-down time provides rich opportunities for sharing between you and your child. You will be able to give your child your full attention and have fun with your child.

Wind-down time between you and your children should take place in a public area of the house, not in the child's bedroom or in yours. This is part of the boundary setting process. Encourage your child to spend some of the wind-down time in his or her room as part of the method of creating positive associations with the sleeping area.

If your child takes a bath or shower before bed, this activity can be done toward the end of the sixty minutes. Soaking in the tub will help relax your child. Bathing and showering are too long to include in the prebedtime prep that will follow wind-down.

Prebedtime Prep

Plan for your child to begin specific preparations for bed immediately following wind-down time and thirty minutes before the set bedtime. As you know, kids often dawdle before bed. So allow thirty minutes to give them plenty of time to get everything done. This way, no one will become frustrated or anxious. It should take less time as the routine becomes automatic.

For the first few minutes, activities include brushing teeth, toileting, washing hands and face, and putting on pajamas. During the remaining time, you and your partner can talk softly with your child or read a story.

Bedtime

When you plan the new bedtime routine, start with a set time for the child to be in the bed and to stay in the bed.

Base the time you set for bed on your child's needs and schedule. You can consult your child's pediatrician to determine how much sleep your child needs depending on age. Work backward from the time you need your child to wake up in the morning and set the bedtime accordingly. If you make the time for bed later on weekends and holidays, it should not vary by more than a half hour.

Sticking to the bedtime you choose is a form of limit setting that clarifies the parent-child boundary. You are the adult who decides what is best for your child; the child is supposed to respect the boundaries you set.

It is generally not a good idea to use or shift the time for bed as a disciplinary tool with your child because doing so will make going to bed punitive rather than pleasant. Deviations from the set bedtime will be random, leading to a loss of the set bedtime and a loss of the structure.

Expect Your Child to Resist the Change

Children at any age are resistant to change. No matter how carefully you plan, your child may put up a fight about sleeping independently, especially if you have been entrenched in the co-sleeping habit for a long time.

Expect and be prepared for the resistance. If you plan to handle the resistance calmly and assertively, your child's discomfort will be less prolonged than if you are inconsistent, upset, angry, or wishy-washy in your approach.

Children this age can be dramatic in their behavior and expression of emotion when they are displeased or if things are done differently from how they want them done. You have probably noticed this already.

Even though by age five your children can make their needs known by talking, they often resort to crying, yelling, or stomping around when upset or displeased. Even ten-year-olds can scream and cry instead of discuss the situation with their good vocabularies.

Overreaction is more common among children who have been sleeping with you for a while. After all, it wasn't their idea to change the sleeping arrangement—it is your idea. But that's okay. You are the parent. You have made the decision—and it hasn't been easy for you—that it is in your child's best interest to break the co-sleeping habit.

This isn't the first—and it certainly isn't the last—parenting decision that your child doesn't like. You will teach your child how to cope with change, now and in the future. Also keep in mind that overreaction to changing the sleep arrangement is also common when children have been rewarded by your giving in to tantrums during the day.

Review the Tools Provided in Chapters 4 and 5

It is of great value to realize in advance of changing your nighttime parenting that your child may tug at your heartstrings, may try very hard to manipulate you—may even threaten you with anger—to keep you in the co-sleeping habit. Anticipate that it will be hard for you not to react by co-sleeping.

Review Chapter 4 on becoming a calm, assertive leader. Remember that you are the leader and decision-maker on what is best for your child's development—not your child, not even a very smart child. Review Chapter 5 on overcoming your inner barriers to change. In particular, fight your impulse to parent with fear and guilt and dispute your powerless thinking.

Plan for Adult Support

In addition to the tools provided in Chapters 4 and 5 to bolster you for the moment of truth, you will also need the support of an adult whom you trust to help you through the first night or two. Plan to get that support before you introduce the new sleep arrangement to your child.

If your spouse or partner is involved, plan to support and encourage each other through the process. If you are in it alone, let a good friend or family member know what you are planning and why it is in your child's best interest. Ask that person to spend that first and second night with you so that you feel supported in the process.

If this is not possible, perhaps a friend or family member would be willing to be available by phone those first two nights so that when you are tempted to give up or need encouragement, you have someone to cheer you on.

If you have not shared with anyone that you and your child co-sleep, this is the time to confide in someone you trust. It is not unusual for parents to feel embarrassed that they still share a bed with one or more children when the children are school age. You may also dread letting anyone see your child upset when you introduce the new bedtime routine. Don't let these internal obstacles stop you from getting the support you will need when you put your plan into action.

Do not hesitate to ask for the support you set up for yourself on that first night. Even if it is very late, in fact, especially if it is very late and you are tired, your child is protesting, and you are doubting your decision to follow through—that's when you need the support the most.

Your willingness to reach out for support for yourself that first night could very well make the difference between succeeding or failing to follow through with your plan to break the co-sleeping habit.

Now that you have a well-thought-out plan and you are mentally and emotionally prepared, you are ready to prepare your child for the important milestone of changing the co-sleeping habit to independent sleep.

Major changes in your children's lives should be accomplished with loving preparation. You want to make sure they are informed in words they understand and that they participate in the process. Their participation will help them own the process of change to independent sleep. The more they own the process, the easier the transition for everyone involved.

There are three steps for preparing your elementary-school-age child for the change from the co-sleeping habit to independent sleep.

The first step is having your child spend time in his or her bedroom during the day. This part of preparing your child begins a week before you put the new bedtime routine into action.

The second step is conducting a family meeting the morning of the first day. It is the evening of that day that you will put your plan, including the new bedtime routine, into action. The purpose of the family meeting is to prepare your child mentally and emotionally for the change to independent sleep.

The third step, which begins immediately after the family meeting is over, is involving your child in getting ready for their first night of independent sleep.

Here are the details on how to prepare your child successfully for changing the co-sleeping habit to independent sleep.

Have Your Child Spend Time in His or Her Bedroom

You want your child to have pleasant, secure associations with the space you have prepared for independent sleep. It takes a little time for new associations to take hold. For children between the ages of five and ten, allow for about one week before beginning independent sleep for your child to adapt to spending more time in his or her bedroom. The time your child spends in the room should be nonthreatening. Do not discuss with your child your plan to break the co-sleeping habit at this time.

Invite your child to spend time enjoying his or her toys, games, and books that you have gathered from other parts of the house and relocated to your child's personal space or room.

If your child asks why he or she is spending more time in the room, tell your child that everyone needs a personal space of their own. Arrange for one of your child's friends to come over for a few hours and encourage the children to play in the designated room. Also encourage your child to spend time alone in the space, engaging in symbolic play, games, or reading.

Your child's clothing should be organized in his or her bedroom during that week before independent sleep begins. Changing clothes after school, before bed, and in the morning should take place in the child's personal space during the week before the target date to implement the new bedtime routine.

Self-care behavior in your child's personal space will promote a sense of privacy for your child that will ease the transition to independent sleep.

It's okay for you to spend time and interact with your child in his or her bedroom. Make sure, though, that when hugging or cuddling, it's not in your child's bed because this would work against your goal of forming new associations.

Conduct a Family Meeting

The best time to inform your child about the new bedtime routine is the morning of the day you will begin independent sleep. Talking with your child any sooner would only trigger anticipatory anxiety. Letting your child know the morning of the same day will give you and your child sufficient time to prepare.

The best format for sharing your plan with your child is the family meeting. It can be helpful to time the meeting for after breakfast at home. Simply remain at the kitchen table after breakfast for the meeting. Make sure that nothing else critical is going on that day. Do not answer the phone, or your cell phone, during the meeting.

If the children in the co-sleeping habit have older siblings who sleep independently, you can either make a prior arrangement for them to be visiting a friend or grandparent or include them in the meeting for support if appropriate.

In a two-parent household, both parents should speak at the meeting. The parent who is the most involved with the child at bedtime should take the lead. Doing so will send the child the message that the co-sleeping parent is committed to making the change and is not being coerced by the other parent. This tactic will also help an overinvolved parent to break through his or her own inhibitions about bringing up the co-sleeping topic with the child. Here are a few tips for the meeting:

- Make sure that each of you has your own space for the meeting.
- The child should not be clinging to anyone or sitting on anyone's lap.
- It's fine if a younger child holds a stuffed animal, but this is not a time for playing with a video game or watching TV. You want your child's full attention.
- Your attitude should be upbeat.

At the start of the meeting, tell your children how proud you are of each of them. Highlight a specific instance in which your child showed independence or growth, for example:

"Jennie, I'm so proud that you are learning to read. It wasn't that long ago that you didn't even know the alphabet. You're really growing up."

"Alec, I was so proud of you yesterday at your baseball game. I can't believe how fast you can run."

"You made some great moves at soccer practice, Maggie. I like the way you listen to your coach."

"I felt so proud when you helped out with Grandma last week, Kenny. You're a great kid!"

The other parent or stepparent can chime in or give the child another compliment.

Next, in a straightforward manner, tell your child that you (or both of you) have decided that your child is now grown up enough for a new plan at bedtime.

Then lay out the basic structure of the plan, including: wind-down time, prebedtime prep, bedtime, and the concept of a separate sleeping space. Let your child know that you will be tucking in and will be at home keeping everyone safe.

Do not mention that you expect protest. If at the mention of the new plan or of the change in routine your child gets up and begins to cling to you, tries to sit on your lap, or whines, it's okay. These are the very behaviors you have seen at bedtime that you are addressing.

Let your child engage in the behavior briefly. Then calmly and assertively, look your child in the eye and lovingly—but with conviction in your voice—redirect your child to the previous state of mind. This is the start of your practicing calm, assertive leadership skills and setting limits for your child.

As soon as things are calm again, tell your child how proud you are and what a good job he or she did. Then continue the description of the plan. Even children who have not yet learned how to tell time have a sense of scheduling activities. Everything during the school day is structured, with activities beginning and ending at specific times. In elementary school, the times for activities and transitions are usually written out for the whole class to see and follow. Your child may be more aware of structure and transitions than you realize.

Tell your child about the prep for bedtime and about the sixty-minute wind-down time. Give examples of some of the fun activities you can do together during wind-down. Tell your child that you will do things together and have fun during wind-down time and that you will help during the prep for bed. Reassure your child that you (and the other parent) will still tuck him or her in, that you will read a story, that you will exchange hugs and kisses, and that then you will say, "Good night."

Whether the co-sleeping habit has taken place in your child's bed or your own, make it clear to your child at the meeting that you know he or she is ready to learn to sleep without you. At this point in the meeting, some children act like it's not a big deal. They don't believe you have it in you to follow through, so the protest won't come until the moment of truth. Other children will protest immediately at the family meeting, at the mere mention of a change in the sleeping arrangement. If your child appears accepting, just leave it at that.

Tips for Family Meeting

- If your child protests, avoid a power struggle.
- Give hugs and reassurance.
- Don't back down and don't postpone putting your plan into action.

Regardless of how your child reacts to the news, provide reassurance at the family meeting that you will help him or her throughout the day by answering questions and doing fun activities to make the new bedtime routine a good experience.

Answer any questions your child has at the moment. More may come up later. The key is to be unwavering but loving and supportive. Then, announce that the family meeting is over.

The Day of the Transition to Independent Sleep

After the family meeting, involve your child immediately in special preparations for the new bedtime plan. Your child's involvement in the process is critical for success. These special preparations will help your child prepare mentally and emotionally for the new bedtime regimen and for independent sleep. All preparations for the first night should be completed prior to wind-down time.

The activities you choose should be consistent with your child's interests and skills. The following is a list of suggested activities. You could:

- Take your child shopping for a new set of sheets, a new pillow, or a new toothbrush. New supplies for grooming and sleeping selected by your child (with your guidance) will signify change and help your child own the process. Using the new sheets or blanket at night that your child had fun selecting will create a positive association for your child at bedtime.
- Ask your child if a nightlight would be helpful. Go with your children into the space you prepared and select the best place for the nightlight. Then, help select a nightlight that appeals to your child. When you get home, plug it in with the lights out and shades drawn to see how it looks.
- Rent a movie that the family can watch together during wind-down time. Make sure that the movie is short enough to end before the set bedtime. Make sure the movie is not scary or overstimulating. Something funny or low-key would be best.
- Get a new game that the family can play together during wind-down time this first evening. A game that encourages cooperation toward a goal or a creative game rather than a wildly competitive game would be best. Avoid video games during wind-down because they are usually overstimulating.
- With kindergarten through second or third grade children, provide construction paper and markers so that you and your child can draw pictures of the prep for bed activities, for example, a toothbrush, a tube of toothpaste, a glass of water, a stuffed animal. Then, hang these pictures on the

bedroom door or in their room as reminders of the activities that need to be accomplished before bedtime.

- With children ages eight through ten years, make a written list of the prebedtime prep activities as a reminder of the components in the routine. Leave room for check marks so that your child can check each item off as it is accomplished.

- You can use a sticker system to encourage compliance with the new bedtime routine. Make a chart with your child and have your child write the days of the week along the side. Your child can pick out stickers that appeal to him or her. Make a plan that each morning you will place a sticker next to the days that your child has successfully fallen asleep and stayed in his or her own bed through the night. The more stickers the child earns each week, the bigger the prize. The prizes don't have to be expensive. They can take the form of privileges.

Keep in mind three key factors about prizes:

1. They have to be important to your child or your child won't work for them.
2. They should not be awarded unless they were earned.
3. Getting to sleep with you on any basis should not be one of the prizes.

Feel free to come up with ideas of your own as a family. Your child might surprise you with good ideas for preparation.

At this point, you have a specific plan, you have your partner's support, and you have prepared your child. You are ready to put your plan into action. Your child will sleep independently tonight. The following sections will describe how to do it.

Keep Track and Stay in Charge

Make sure that you follow your plan. It is essential to initiate the new routine on time and to keep track of the time. Initiate wind-down time at the time you planned. By doing so, your child will see that you are following through with the plan. This perception will help your child be prepared for the rest of the plan, including independent sleep. If you let the time slip away and forfeit winding down, your chances of reaching your ultimate goal will be reduced. Say to your child (and to your partner if he or she needs reminding) that it's time to wind down. Remember, if you watch TV with your child, choose a show that is family oriented or funny, not action or scary.

When you first introduce the new routine, it will feel inconvenient to your child. Children this age do not welcome change. But through practicing the routine night after night, your child will experience the comfort of the repetition and ritual and will want to incorporate it into the fabric of daily life.

Initiate Prebedtime Prep

You have gone over this with your child. Your child may have drawn pictures of it. So it is not a surprise. On this first night of the new routine, help your child, but do not hover. You and your child have thirty minutes to get through a few simple tasks. If the routine takes less time, then the remaining time can be used to continue to wind down in your child's bedroom.

Tuck In for Independent Sleep

Tuck your child in as soon as he or she has completed the pre-bedtime prep. Tucking in should take about fifteen to twenty minutes. This first night, allow an extra five or ten minutes for providing comfort and support and for encouraging your child to use self-comforting techniques.

Your goal for tucking in is to reassure your child that he or she is loved and safe. Before your child is in bed and under the covers, make sure that:

- All of his or her bathroom needs have been met.
- Your child has water available near the bed.
- There is no further need for your child to leave the bed for the night.

Set Limits

When tucking in, sit at the edge of the bed or on a chair next to the bed while your child is under the covers. Do not get under the covers with your child. Don't lie down with your child, no matter what. If you do, the process is doomed to failure.

Remember that the process of tucking in has a beginning, middle, and an end. Prolonging the time and never ending the tucking-in process does not provide further reassurance. Limit the reading to one story or to a few pages from a chapter book. Older children can read out loud as you listen if that is their preference.

Provide Comfort and Support

Your child will need extra comfort and support on this first night, and maybe for the next few nights.

You may rub your child's back or arms when you read or talk together. Gentle massaging will make most children sleepy. Do not massage until your child falls asleep or your child will continue to need massaging during partial awakenings.

If your child wants to talk about the change that's occurring, gently remind him or her about what you discussed at the family meeting that day and of the preparations made for this important night.

Tell your child with a loving, confident tone of voice: "I know you'll be fine sleeping without me," or "Sleeping by yourself is an important part of growing up." Make sure your behavior and tone communicate this message: *You are safe.*

Encourage Your Child to Self-Comfort

Children this age already know how to self-comfort. For example, when children have to go to the bathroom in school but have to wait a few minutes, they use self-comforting techniques to cope while waiting. When children raise their hand to answer a question in class but do not get called on, they self-comfort to deal with it. When a friend is not available when a child wants to play, he or she self-comforts. You can probably think of many more examples. During those times, children tell themselves some form of "It's okay. I can deal with it."

Tonight, your child will have the opportunity to apply self-comforting tools to the sleeping situation. Remind your child of situations in which you have noticed him or her self-comfort. Ask about it. Let your child explain how he or she used self-comforting to feel better when stressed about something. Teach your child how to apply the same words or techniques to learning how to sleep without you.

Younger children might find that a favorite stuffed animal or other soft object in the bed can provide comfort. A nightlight can provide comfort for children of any age.

A bottle of water next to the bed helps children relax. Some children are comforted by singing to themselves. Thinking about the rewards that can be earned through the sticker system can be comforting for your child.

You can allow your older elementary-school-age child to read for a few minutes after you leave the room. Imagining a peaceful scene, like the beach, is a good self-comforting tool for your child, too. You might want to read the section in Chapter 8 on Relaxation Techniques for your older child in this age group.

Disengage after Tucking In

Disengagement is the signal that tucking in has ended. It sets the limit. It is the hardest part of tucking in for you and your child if you have been entrenched in the co-sleeping habit. Disengagement is the part of tucking in you have not achieved before. But you can achieve it now. This is how to disengage:

- Make sure the self-comforting tools are in place.
- Get and give your last hug and kiss.
- Turn out the light and say, "Goodnight."
- Leave the room.

Disengagement is the point at which the process of breaking the co-sleeping habit may have fallen apart in the past for you and your child. That's because it is difficult to leave the room when your child is upset. It is essential for breaking the co-sleeping habit that you leave the room even if your child is upset. No matter what your child says or does when you begin to disengage, do not be conned into "one more story," or one more drink or snack, and most importantly, do not lie down with your child.

If you want to reassure your child more than you already have, make one or two reassuring statements. Make sure when you comfort your child that your tone matches your words.

Here are some examples of what you could say:

- If your child talks about being afraid of monsters, simply say: "There's no such thing as monsters. You're okay."

- "I will protect you even when I'm not in your room. I will (or the other parent will) be in the house."
- "You are ready to have your own personal sleeping space."
- "You can read a book for a few minutes."
- "Tell yourself you'll be okay."
- "I know you'll be okay falling asleep without me. I'll see you in the morning."

Once you've made your statements, leave the room even if your child is upset. Remind yourself that you have been a loving, supportive parent tonight. Here's the evidence:

- You have prepared your child for a week, and intensively for a whole day.
- Your child has participated in getting ready for this moment.
- You have made your child physically comfortable.
- You have provided reassurance and support.
- You have reminded your child how to self-comfort.
- You have tucked your child in.

So—it's really okay to leave the room now even if your child disagrees. Your child's difficulty with the idea of sleeping without you means that your child really needs your help to disengage. Your giving in at this point would not only be a setback, but you would also be prolonging your child's upset in the long run.

Give Yourself Comfort and Encouragement

At this point, you might have to give yourself comforting messages as well. To help yourself leave your child's room and stay out, dispute the negative thoughts in your head that make you feel guilty.

Examine Your Self-Talk

When you hear yourself think, *I'm making my child suffer*, respond to yourself with:

- My child will suffer more in the long run if I continue to enable this dependency.
- I am helping my child through a normal transition.
- I am being a responsible, loving parent.

Remember, you have prepared your child, you have provided wind-down time, you have made comforting statements, and you have encouraged self-comfort. Be patient.

Reach Out for the Support You Planned

In addition to giving yourself comforting and rational self-talk, look for support and encouragement from your partner or friend you have chosen to help you during the first few nights.

Don't Blame Your Child for Your Actions

This is the point at which parents often tell themselves, "My child won't let me leave the room." Remember from Chapter 5, stop blaming your child for your behavior. Your child doesn't want you to leave the room because you and your child have been caught up in a habit. But you are changing the habit. After tucking in your child, reassuring your child, and encouraging self-comfort, you need to give your child space and time to learn how to cope with falling asleep.

How to Deal with Your Child's Protests

After you disengage, your child may cry or call out to you. Your child may whine, beg, bargain, or get angry. Check in briefly. Then leave. Wait for at least two minutes, three if you can. Then, without reacting to what your child said or to your child's emotionality, look in very briefly (twenty to thirty seconds) and say calmly: "Everything is okay. You can express yourself if you need to, but do your best to fall asleep because you need your rest." Then, leave, even if your child is upset or talking to you. Your leaving sends positive messages:

- You meant it about getting their rest.
- You can be trusted to follow through.
- You are letting your children know they are safe in their room with you somewhere else in the house.

Follow Through

Your child may continue to cry, scream, and carry on to the point of sounding desperate when not getting his or her own way. Children this age are known to make extreme emotional verbal statements. If you give in and reinforce your child's irrational behavior and statements with verbal acknowledgment, your child may continue this type of maneuver night after night.

The best way to deal with begging, bargaining, anger, and other forms of manipulative verbal behavior is to ignore it. If you become engaged in interaction with your child when your child behaves this way, you will either give in, lose your temper, cry, or do something else that makes you fail your child's test to see if you really are a calm, assertive leader who knows what is best and who is equipped to keep your child safe.

If your child expresses anger, the anger is really discomfort about change. As your child learns to use self-comforting techniques, the anger will evaporate. Your child still loves you even when saying, "I hate you."

Keep in mind that in addition to acting desperately, your child may ask "Why?" about a topic to the point of wearing you out and may argue as well as any defense attorney. He or she is capable of continuous arguing, begging, and proposing deals, both realistic and outrageous.

Avoid Power Struggles

This is not the time to respond or to compromise. Any type of verbal response on your part will just prolong the interaction and turn the situation into a power struggle. It is important that you not get drawn into a power struggle with your child after tucking in. You need to give your child the time he or she needs to learn how to use the self-comforting techniques you talked about when tucking in.

Let's say you ignore the behavior initially and then respond after forty-five minutes of protest to your child's demand for interaction or for more water or for any delay tactic. You will not be comforting your child. Rather, you will be conditioning your child to carry on for that length of time to get your response. If you respond after two hours, you will be conditioning the child to carry on for two hours to get your response.

To achieve your goal, you must ignore the behavior. This does not mean that you ignore your child.

Check In When Your Child Is Quiet

As your child is learning how to cope with the tools you have provided, you will be checking in with your child. Check in when there is a moment of quiet.

Checking in means entering the room briefly without doing anything for the child. You're just making it known that you are around. It is important not to touch the child when you are checking in.

The no touching is important because if you touch after tucking in, your child will look for your touch throughout the night during partial awakenings rather than learn to self-comfort. Also, your touching without staying is a tease that can set off protest when you leave the room again after checking in. In other words, touching at this point may comfort you at the moment, but it can set off more upset in your child and will make it harder on your child as the night progresses.

Keep the Checking In Brief

Seeing you for twenty to thirty seconds, without your having to say or do anything, is reassuring. You are making the statement by checking in that you are there, in the house, that you are keeping your child safe. You are developing your child's ability to be comforted by a distal stimulus (seeing you) without needing a proximal stimulus (touching) for comfort as your child learns how to self-comfort.

You may spend an hour or more proving that you are really available. Make sure you check in when your child is quiet. If you're consistent and follow the plan, your child will eventually fall asleep.

Getting Your Child Back to Bed

Don't go to bed until your child is asleep. Stay in a nearby room—not your bedroom. If your child comes out to find you, escort him or her back to bed.

The first time it happens, say, "It's bedtime." After that, no matter how many times your child gets out of bed, whether it is to go to your bedroom or to another room, escort back with no reward.

It is important that there be no interaction, no cuddling, and no rewards of any kind. Your voice is a reward. Don't use it. If you provide affection, snacks, water, or anything else reinforcing, the behavior will continue night after night. Do not give in to any demands.

Maintain a matter-of-fact demeanor with no reinforcement for as many times as it takes. This consistent, nonrewarding action on your part is key to your child's learning to fall asleep and stay asleep without co-sleeping.

Your child may pop out of bed several times. You may need the emotional support of your partner or friend to win this power struggle. If at any point you reinforce the behavior of getting out of bed by giving in to your child's request for something, you are conditioning your child to get out the number of times it took to get that reward. Even though you may feel like it will never happen, your child will eventually stay in bed and fall asleep.

If your child sneaks into your room or your bed in the middle of the night, escort him or her back to bed immediately. You can no longer remain "unaware" that your child has entered your bed. The first time this happens, say to your child, "It's past your bedtime." After that, take the child back to his or her bed with no interaction.

You're tired. But this effort up front will pay off. Your child will learn not only to fall asleep without you, but also to stay asleep without you. Sleeping through the whole night will provide your child (and you) restorative sleep that is necessary for optimal functioning and good health. If you give in and let your child stay with you in your bed, you'll be back to square one. After all the planning, effort, and progress you have made so far in breaking the co-sleeping habit, it's worth it to go the distance.

Follow Through No Matter How Long It Takes

You must follow through that first night no matter how long it takes. If you give in and lie down or sleep with your child now, you will give your child the messages that (1) your words have no meaning, (2) it really is unsafe to sleep independently, (3) you have no faith in your child's coping skills, and (4) it is okay with you that your child controls you and the family.

If you give in at any point, you will condition your child to engage in all the behavior that preceded your giving in, thus causing the co-sleeping habit to become more deeply entrenched.

Get Some Rest and Stop Worrying

When your child is finally asleep, it is time for you to get some rest and stop worrying. You and your child have made it through the first big hurdle. You did not react to your child's upset by co-sleeping. You gave your child the time and space to self-comfort. Your child proved to you—and more importantly to himself or herself—that he or she can fall asleep without you. Now you can get some rest and think about how proud you are that your child accomplished a significant developmental milestone tonight. Know that your child will still love you and be bonded to you in the morning.

Maintaining Gains

You and your child have achieved a milestone. To maintain the gains you have made in breaking the co-sleeping habit, you need to build on that success.

Praise and Reassure

In the morning, wake your child up at the usual time. Make sure that you praise your child for falling asleep and staying asleep without you.

If after being praised or later that day your child broaches the subject of wanting to sleep with you tonight, be calm and assertive as you tell your child that you will continue to help him or her to sleep without you. Involve your child in getting the bed made in the morning as preparation. Older elementary school children should learn to make their own bed as part of their morning routine.

Repetition Will Reinforce New Habits

Repeat the new bedtime routine and your other strategies for independent sleep each night until your child is sleeping independently with no fuss. This may take a few days or a week. From time to time, your child may continue to test you, and you will pass the test and make your child feel secure if you continue to provide the same structure, reassurance, and self-comforting tools.

Remember that your child will respond to the structure, repetition, and ritual you are providing. Within a few nights, your child will need less verbal reassurance and will settle down more easily as he or she discovers internal resources for coping.

New Sleep Associations Will Form

Over the next few nights, your child will begin to form new sleep associations at bedtime and no longer associate falling asleep with having you available to touch. Your younger child will associate falling asleep with holding a cherished stuffed animal or a soft blanket or seeing a soothing nightlight. Your older child will be able to self-comfort with positive self-talk and soothing mental images, or reading before falling asleep.

When he or she partially wakes during the night, as we all do, your child will be able to fall back into a sound sleep, rather than wake up fully, because the same conditions that were present when originally falling asleep will be available throughout the night. Your child will rely on you less—and rely on himself or herself more—for falling asleep and staying asleep over the next few nights.

Further Tips

On school nights, everyone will be busier, so plan to ensure adequate time for wind-down and the prebedtime prep. Wind-down should not be sacrificed because of busy schedules.

During the bedtime routine on the nights that follow, encourage more independence during the prebedtime prep. By age five, your child should be able to change from daytime clothing to pajamas without assistance, put daytime clothes into the hamper, and brush teeth fairly quickly.

If you are consistent, within a week, the co-sleeping habit will be broken and the new bedtime routine followed by independent sleep will take hold.

CHAPTER 8

How to Intervene with Preteens and Teens

Although the co-sleeping habit with preteens and teens is less common than it is with younger children, it affects a significant number of families. In some families, the co-sleeping habit with preteens and teens has existed for many years, from infancy or early childhood. It may have started with the family bed that had no exit plan. Or it may have started with parents' continually reinforcing their young child's protest to sleeping alone. In other families, the habit began later in the child's life in reaction to an event, such as a divorce. The co-sleeping habit can also take hold when parents co-sleep to soothe the symptoms of their adolescent's anxiety disorder.

With all children, toddlers through teens, the planning and implementation of the plan to break the co-sleeping habit is up to the parents. With toddlers and preschoolers, the process is completely parent driven. By elementary school, children need to be more actively involved in owning the process of breaking the co-sleeping habit than are toddlers or preschoolers, but the process is still driven by parent directives.

Breaking the co-sleeping habit with teens and preteens is more of a partnership. Children at this age can think on a more abstract level than younger children and are capable of more self-control.

As parents, you are still guiding and monitoring the process of breaking the co-sleeping habit, but with a child between the ages of eleven through eighteen, your child's active involvement, self-monitoring, and motivation are essential to success.

If your preteen or younger teen has been slow to mature emotionally and socially, you have the option of following the plan for breaking the co-sleeping habit for elementary school children presented in the previous chapter. Read both that chapter and this chapter for teens and preteens and decide for yourselves. Remember to trust your judgment as a parent and use the techniques that you feel are the best fit for your child and situation.

Sometimes It's Easy

Charlie, age thirteen, routinely co-slept with his mother while his father slept alone in the den. Charlie's parents brought their son into their bed when he developed asthma as a preschooler. Beginning in Charlie's kindergarten year, his dad began sleeping in the living room, and Charlie and his mom remained in the co-sleeping habit and stayed there.

Charlie's poor impulse control during the day led to multiple school suspensions. He did not see himself as having to abide by limits.

Charlie and his parents became involved in counseling because of his behavior problems in school. Through counseling, Charlie's parents recognized that the poor boundaries in the household, including the co-sleeping habit, had to be changed in order for Charlie's daytime behavior to improve.

Charlie's parents decided that they wanted to reclaim their marital relationship as well as their status as authority figures in the family. They began that process with their decision to change the sleeping arrangement.

They chose a quiet time during the evening to share with Charlie that they thought it was time to straighten out the sleeping arrangement, that Mom and Dad wanted to be together in their bedroom and that it would be better for him to have his own private space.

His parents sat near each other, showing that they were together on this issue, as they shared their feelings calmly with Charlie. Then they asked him what he thought about or felt about the idea. They weren't sure what to expect.

To their surprise, Charlie responded, "Okay."

And that was it. Rather than elaborate or dissect the situation any further at the moment, his mom responded, "Great. Come and help me freshen up your room."

Charlie went to bed in his own room that night without a problem.

As the days passed and the situation normalized, Charlie's mom asked him how he felt about sleeping in his own room. His response was, "It's fine. I would've done it sooner, but I thought you needed me with you."

Even though it's not always that easy, sometimes it is. Many teens and preteens are ready to sleep on their own, but no one has brought it up. This was the case with Tammy, age sixteen, who was in the co-sleeping habit with her mom.

Tammy and her mom seemed more like sisters than mother and daughter. Her mom was flattered when anyone had that opinion. They spent a lot of time together shopping, watching TV, and exercising. Tammy's mom, who never married, was only seventeen when she had her. Tammy had never met her father, who was described by her mom as "out of the picture."

Tammy and her mom always co-slept. The co-sleeping was a habit based on mom's enmeshment with her daughter. Without realizing it, Tammy's mom came to depend on Tammy as her friend, her confidante—her whole world. The co-sleeping, rather than creating security for Tammy, was burdening and suffocating her.

Neither of them realized the extent of the problem until the middle of high school when Tammy became depressed. Although mom never restricted Tammy by telling her she could not participate with her peers, Tammy felt guilty leaving her mom alone for soccer tournaments, dances, or time with her friends. Dating seemed out of the question. Tammy began to change from an outgoing, fun-loving child to a quiet, reserved, sullen teenager. At times, she had angry outbursts over nothing. Her mother became concerned and called a therapist.

Through the process of counseling, it became apparent that the overinvolvement was harmful emotionally for both Tammy and her mother. The first intervention was to break the co-sleeping habit. Tammy had a bedroom, but there was no bed in it. Both she and her mom used it as an office.

During a mother-daughter counseling session, Tammy's mom asked Tammy how she would feel about their setting up the second bedroom as her bedroom. Tammy's face lit up. She then squelched her enthusiasm and said that she saw no reason to do that. It was apparent that she felt guilty about her own enthusiasm about having her own space, and possibly her own life.

The therapist encouraged Tammy's mom to see through her daughter's words and to let Tammy know that she felt it would be good for both of them. After making sure that it was really okay with her mom, Tammy began planning what to do to convert the room, color patterns and all.

Tammy and her mom went shopping for the bed and the bedding and decorated the room together, according to Tammy's taste. The co-sleeping habit was broken, and the bond between Tammy and her mother was healthier.

The cases of Charlie and Tammy illustrate something significant about the co-sleeping habit that I have seen many times as a therapist. The co-sleeping may have begun early in the child's life as a well-intentioned way to protect the child. In Charlie's case, his mom wanted to protect him from the danger of an asthma attack in the middle of the night. In Tammy's case, her mom wanted to protect her from feeling abandoned by her father. But in both cases, these parents began to rely on their children for emotional support. The switch from protecting their children to their children fulfilling the parents' needs was gradual, unintentional, and undetected, but it led to the co-sleeping habit and role confusion in the family. The fallout was that these children felt burdened and they had difficulty adjusting to the developmental tasks of adolescence.

If your are a parent in this type of situation and you make it clear to your preteens and teens that they are entitled to their own space and that you're truly okay with that, then breaking the co-sleeping habit will be easy for them. As you see your child function better emotionally and you begin to expand your life outside of being a parent, breaking the co-sleeping habit will have been worth it for *you* as well.

The Preteen or Teen Who Won't Fall Asleep Alone

Sometimes, it's not so easy. The co-sleeping habit that takes the form of lying down with your child until he or she falls asleep can go on and on and on through the years.

Kate, age eleven, insisted since she was a preschooler that her mom stay with her until she fell asleep. After many failed attempts to convince Kate that she'd be okay to fall asleep on her own, her mom gave in and stayed with her every night, in her bed.

If her mom tried to sneak out and Kate wasn't fully asleep, Kate protested, and her mom reacted by staying longer. After Kate turned six years old, her mom stopped trying to separate before Kate was fully asleep. She felt that Kate just wasn't capable of falling asleep on her own. Some nights, Kate's mom waited until she was sure her daughter was sound asleep and then went to bed. Several nights a week, she fell asleep in Kate's bed, woke up at 2 or 3 A.M. and then went back to the marital bed. There were many nights that Kate woke up during the night, discovered her mom "missing," and crawled into her parents' bed.

After years of interrupted sleep, lack of adult time in the evening, and the realization that Kate was controlling her in the daytime as well, Kate's mom decided it was time to break the co-sleeping habit. Kate's dad had wanted the situation to change for a long time, so he was already on board.

One Saturday morning after breakfast, Kate's parents sat down with her for a talk. They did not tell her that the situation would have to change or that they had a plan to change it because they knew she would freak out and the discussion would be over. Instead, they approached her by validating her maturity and asking open-ended questions that they thought would not engage her defenses.

Her dad validated her maturity by telling her how proud he was of her good sense of direction, of the good judgment she showed when a stray dog showed up in the yard, and of how she resolved a conflict with her best friend.

Her mom asked her how she felt about having a sleepover party. When Kate hesitated, her mom expressed confidence that Kate could handle it. Her mom gently broached the subject of the co-sleeping issue by asking Kate what she thought she needed to learn in order to fall asleep on her own.

Through calm discussion and gentle questioning, Kate began to open up. The issue was not forced. Kate talked about not liking how her bed was situated in the room because she could not see into the hallway. She talked about almost falling asleep but then waking up.

Her parents offered to help her with these issues when she was ready. In the meantime, the arrangement stayed the same. But Kate became uneasy about keeping things the same. The discussion made Kate think about the discrepancy in her mature behavior and judgments during the day and her acting like a baby at bedtime.

About a week later, Kate brought up the subject, and Kate and her parents made a plan to rearrange the furniture in her bedroom so that she could see into the hallway. Her mother learned about and taught Kate relaxation techniques so that she could fall asleep more easily. Kate participated in a partnership with her parents to break the co-sleeping habit.

Calm, loving discussion and the use of relaxation techniques also helped Jonathan, a fifteen-year-old high school freshman whose grandfather lay with him in bed each night until Jonathan dozed off. Jonathan came to live with his grandparents at age twelve, when his mother went into rehab for drug addiction. After a prolonged treatment, she relapsed, and now no one knows where she is. Jonathan's father drops in to see his son from time to time, but he is not in a position to provide him with a home.

Jonathan is a good student, a good athlete, and good citizen. He is bonded with his grandparents but doesn't talk too much about his feelings.

Jonathan's grandparents always had a bedroom for him because even before he came to live with them, his mother would drop him off for prolonged periods of time without notice. His grandfather would tell him stories at bedtime, and Jonathan would drift off to sleep. However, when Jonathan came to live with them permanently, he would ask his grandfather to stay with him until he fell asleep. He said he just couldn't shut off his mind. His grandfather complied with the request, figuring it was a short-term problem. But night after night, Jonathan begged his grandfather to stay, and he did. He felt bad that Jonathan was essentially abandoned by both his parents. Over three years, Jonathan and his grandfather became entrenched in the co-sleeping habit.

Now that Jonathan was in high school, his grandparents decided it was time for Jonathan to learn to fall asleep on his own. He had always done so when he was younger. They felt that they were holding him back from growing into the independent young man they knew he could be. So they had a talk with him.

They told him how proud they were of his accomplishments, making the honor roll and writing for the school newspaper. They told him how much they were impressed by his maturity and good character, for example, when he turned in a wallet he found on the floor of the grocery store. Then they gently brought up the subject of his parents.

They told him that his parents' problems were their own problems, that he didn't cause them and that he couldn't fix them. They told him how they loved him as though he was their own son, and doubly so because he was their grandson. They asked him how they could help him learn how to fall asleep after being tucked in, the way he used to when he was a younger child.

Through their open, loving discussion, the family decided to learn relaxation techniques that Jonathan could use at bedtime to help him fall asleep. Through their reassurance and teaching Jonathan how to relax his mind and body at bedtime, this family was successful in breaking the co-sleeping habit.

If you have a preteen or teenager who won't fall asleep without you, you can engage your child in a partnership to change this habit. To head off defensiveness and resistance, don't insist that the situation must change. Approach your child in a gentle, but focused discussion in which you:

- Express pride in his or her accomplishments and character with examples.
- Validate his or her maturity with examples.
- Ask open-ended questions and ask for suggestions on how to help.

- Make it emotionally safe for your preteen or teen to open up.
- Give your teen and preteen a little time to come to you.

When your child is on board, your learning and then teaching relaxation techniques can help your teen or preteen fall asleep without you.

Relaxation Techniques to Help Your Teen or Preteen Fall Asleep

Before teaching someone else to do something, it makes sense to learn how to do it for yourself. Once you know how to use relaxation techniques properly, you can teach them to your adolescent. Relaxation techniques have helped millions of people relax their bodies and minds sufficiently to fall asleep

The mind and the body have an ongoing relationship. If you use a technique to relax your body, mental relaxation will follow. If you use a technique to relaxing your mind, your body will relax, too. It's the way we're constructed. Keep three things in mind:

1.   Some techniques work better for some people than others. One type of exercise might work better for you, while another works better for your child. So keep an open mind.

2.   Learning to relax is a skill. When you first try a relaxation technique on yourself and later for your child, there may be interrupting thoughts, focusing might not come easily, or you or they might feel silly. With practice, the skill to relax will improve.

3.   Your goal is for your teen or preteen to eventually use the relaxation techniques that work best for them on their own as a

tool for falling asleep independently and for getting back to sleep during the partial awakenings during the night.

Breathing

Breathing is something we all do automatically. We don't have to think about breathing to stay alive. However, when tense, our breathing becomes shallow. When this happens, anxious feelings are almost inevitable.

The following technique is designed to help you, and your child, to take "normal" breaths, instead of shallow breaths, while trying to fall asleep. It is very simple.

- Start with one deep breath and let it out slowly. Just one.
- Then, breathe normally, not too deep and not too shallow. Try to breathe evenly with each breath like the one just before it.
- Count your breaths silently on each exhale. Breathe in and then as you exhale think, "One." Breathe in again and as you exhale, think "Two." Continue counting your exhales until your reach ten. Then, notice how you feel. You should feel more relaxed.

If you find it was helpful, you can do it again, counting your breaths from one through ten. Make sure your breathing is normal, not too deep and not too shallow.

Doing this exercise can regulate your breathing, which will help you relax as you are in bed trying to fall asleep. Focusing on counting your breaths helps you stop thinking about other things.

Once you have mastered this relaxation technique, teach it to your preteen or teen, just as it is described here. Once your child has mastered it, he or she can easily practice it without you when trying to fall asleep.

Progressive Relaxation

Falling asleep can be difficult if your muscles are tense. Tension can become so much of a habit that you don't even realize that your muscles are tense. This exercise is designed to make you and your child more aware of muscle tension as a way to reduce it and to relax muscle groups one at a time.

As you lie in bed, tense your fists as hard as you can. Hold them in that tense position for five to seven seconds, and then release them completely and take a breath. Feel the relaxation in your hands.

Now tense your arms and shoulders as hard as you can. Hold them in that tense position for five to seven seconds, and then release them completely and take a breath. Feel the relaxation in your arms and shoulders.

Now, tense your stomach as hard as you can. Do the hold, the release, and take a breath as you did with your hands, arms, and shoulders.

You can do as many body parts as you wish using the same progression. You will feel each part of your body relax. This will help your mind relax as well and help you fall asleep.

Once you have mastered the progressive relaxation technique, teach it to your preteen or teen. Speak in a gentle voice as you go through each body part with the specific instructions provided above. After guiding your child through relaxing his or her muscle groups, ask him or her to mentally scan the body for any remaining areas of bodily tension. If any are identified, repeat the instructions for that muscle group.

This progressive relaxation exercise can be done after the breathing exercise or by itself. With a little practice, your child should be able to use this technique without you for falling asleep.

Mental Imagery

Guiding yourself, and then after you have mastered it, guiding your preteen or teen, to use mental imagery as a relaxation tool is a great way to fall asleep. Being able to focus on something other than the clutter in your mind is a skill that can take time to develop. The first step is to apply the breathing exercise described above. Once the body is calm, it is easier to focus the mind on calming images. Different images work for different people. What works for your child may be different from what works for you. Here are some suggested images:

> *Imagine a safe place. It could be a real place or a make-believe place. It's a place you can go to in your mind where you feel calm and relaxed. Imagine being in your safe place. Imagine how you feel, what you see and hear, how it smells. Breathe evenly and enjoy taking your mind to your safe place.*

Here's a different image:

> *Count the colors in a rainbow. . . . Watch a beautiful sunset over a body of water. . . . Imagine a country lake in the summertime. . . . Imagine that same lake in the winter . . . in the fall when the leaves are turning. . . . Imagine a colorful campfire. . . . Imagine feeling the warmth from that campfire. . . . Imagine your whole body feeling calm and relaxed.*

Here's another image:

> *Imagine a beautiful flower right in front of you. . . . Imagine the colors in that flower. . . . Imagine your whole mind filled with the colors in the flower. . . . Look at those colors as you let your mind and body relax.*

When you try the mental imagery with your children, ask them which images are the most relaxing. They might come up with other ideas for mental imagery that help them relax in their beds so that they can fall asleep on their own.

These relaxation techniques can help elementary school children as well.

When to Seek Professional Help

Suzie, age seventeen, is a high school senior. At a time in her life when her parents expected her to become more independent, she seemed to be relying on them more. She had always been a little clingy and nervous, but her struggle to cope was increasing with age rather than resolving itself. Suzie was becoming more flustered than ever when trying to make simple decisions like which sweater to wear in the morning. She would go back and forth so many times and kept changing her clothes so many times that she would be late for school. If her mom or dad encouraged her to make up her mind, she would cry and panic as though the pressure was too much for her.

She began to retreat from social activities. She expressed anxiety about catching a disease if she went to a party, not knowing what to say when meeting new people, and her parents getting injured at home while she was out. Suzie began to spend more time in her room reading and less time interacting or participating.

Her worry and avoidance during the day affected her sleep. Her parents tucked her in every night, as they always had. She struggled to fall asleep and slept fitfully, waking up about every half hour. By the middle of the night, she had worked herself into a panic and lay in bed worrying. She worried about failing in school, even though she was an A/B student. She worried about her parents dying, even though they were young and in good health. She worried about the house burning down, even though it was made of brick and had smoke alarms. She worried about dying from carbon monoxide poisoning, even though nothing in the house was powered by gas. She worried over minutia, as well, like what if by accident she wore a tee shirt without realizing it had a stain on it.

For the past six months, with all these thoughts spinning in her head at night, she would wake up her mom and ask her if they could talk. Her mom would sit with her in the family room and try to convince her that her worry was excessive. Suzie would not be convinced. Her mother learned relaxation techniques and taught them to Suzie. Suzie could not concentrate on her breathing or on soothing images. Her mind was too cluttered. Her mom would eventually lie in Suzie's bed with her until morning to make sure she got enough sleep to function in school the next day. The interrupted sleep and concern about not being able to help her daughter took its toll on Suzie's mother.

On those nights that her mom was too exhausted, Suzie's dad tried to comfort her. He would lie down on top of the covers at the foot of Suzie's bed until morning, hoping that his presence would comfort her. And it did at the time. But the next day, nothing would change. He went to work exhausted. And Suzie's anxiety continued to escalate, day and night. Suzie began to have stomachaches almost daily, but the doctor could find no physical cause. Already petite and slender, Suzie began to eat less and lose weight. Her parents didn't know what to do. The co-sleeping habit in Suzie's case was a symptom of a larger problem that the family could not solve on their own. Their next step was to seek professional help.

Derek, age fourteen, has always been a sensitive, loving boy. He would be the one to immediately come to the aid of a classmate who got hurt playing a game. He would be the one to ask his mom if she was okay if he knew she wasn't feeling well earlier.

Increasingly, his sensitivity and caring turned to worry. At first, he worried about little things, like whether he would have enough time to finish a school project. But as he got older, he worried about more remote things, for example, when his dad was a half hour late coming home, he worried he had been killed or kidnapped. He called his dad numerous times at his office to make sure he was okay. He began to stay home more in case something bad happened or in case one of his parents or his younger brother needed his help for an emergency. His brother, who was a year younger than Derek, was not a worrier. He couldn't understand why Derek worried so much about everything.

Derek's excessive worry extended into bedtime. What if someone tries to break and enter into the house? What if the furnace explodes? What if someone dies while sleeping?

When Derek was a young child, he had difficulty falling asleep, but with support and reassurance, he was able to sleep independently on most nights until he was about twelve years old.

Starting in seventh grade, when most children become more independent, Derek regressed. He seemed to need his parents' support more and more. But no matter how much reassurance they gave him, he would always come up with another "What if?"

For the past two years, Derek slept with his parents in their bed. He would sleep right in between them. His brother slept independently in his own room without any problem.

When Derek's parents took steps to break the co-sleeping habit, Derek began to have what looked to them like panic attacks. They didn't know what to do. His mom talked with the guidance counselor at school to get a referral for a good therapist in the community.

In the cases of Suzie and Derek, the co-sleeping habit is part of a larger problem in which sleep disturbance in just one symptom. Most children experience anxiety or insomnia from time to time. As you know as the parent of a preteen or teenager, the stressors can be great for your children. Some worry is normal. But if your child cannot be soothed, if your child's worries seem excessive and interfere with their daytime functioning and their ability to fall asleep and stay asleep, you would be wise to seek professional help. Getting into and staying entrenched in the co-sleeping habit is not a solution that can work for your child long term.

It is important not to diagnose your child on your own. As tempting as it is to try to figure out what is wrong by reading articles on the Internet, it is easy to jump to conclusions and develop fears of your own, which will only make matters worse. There are many types of anxiety disorders and other emotional problems that affect preteens and teens. The best thing to do if you find yourself in the co-sleeping habit with a preteen or teen whose anxiety, worry, or depression seems over the top is to consult a therapist. If the therapist wants you to be involved in the treatment process, make the time to do it. Sometimes combining individual therapy for your child with family therapy can yield excellent results.

CHAPTER 9

How to Deal with Special Situations

This book has provided you with guidance and specific instruction on how to break the co-sleeping habit with your children, toddlers through teens. You have been shown how to become a calm, assertive leader who makes plans for raising your children rather than reacting moment to moment. You have been given the tools to identify and change your inner barriers so that you can follow through effectively with your parenting plan to break the co-sleeping habit. This chapter will give you answers to your questions on how to deal with the co-sleeping habit in special situations that may not have been covered by the preceding chapters.

Breaking the Co-Sleeping Habit with More Than One Child

For many families who engage in the co-sleeping habit, there is more than one child involved. It may not be every child in the household, it may be two out of three or a different number, but it can certainly be more than one.

Suppose you are co-sleeping with more than one child, and they are different ages. Do you break the co-sleeping habit all at once with all of them or one at a time? If it's one at a time, where do you begin, with the oldest or youngest?

There is no one right answer on procedure. But let's sort it out in the most logical way. Let's say they're all in your bed and you have decided that you are ready to reclaim your bed and you want your children to sleep in their own rooms. You probably wish you could wave a magic wand, and poof! Everyone is content in their own sleeping spaces. However, you know it's not that simple. Consider the following options. Be sure to think through the process and plan carefully if you are breaking the co-sleeping habit with more than one child.

- You can start with the child that you believe is ready to move into his or her own bed. You know your children well enough to decide who that is. That child may be the youngest, oldest, or in between. If you begin with the child who is ready for independent sleep, this will free you up for breaking the co-sleeping habit with the more challenging children.
- You can start with the oldest and work your way down, and then enlist the aid of the older children as role models and as extra leverage as you break the co-sleeping habit with your younger children.
- You can start with the younger children. As your older children observe their younger siblings coping with falling asleep and staying asleep on their own, they may follow suit and decide not to be shown up by their younger siblings.
- If the children who co-sleep with you are close in age, you could try breaking the co-sleeping habit with them at the same time. The strategies would be the same within the age group and they could learn from each other. For

elementary school children, you can conduct just one family meeting for preparation if more than one child in that age group is in the co-sleeping habit with you.

When Your Children Are in the Co-Sleeping Habit with Each Other

You have provided a comfortable bed for each one of your children, but they choose to sleep together. Or maybe a younger child crawls into bed with an older child in the middle of the night and your older child is not too happy about it.

If one child occasionally sleeps with a sibling for fun or for comfort during a storm, for example, that's not a problem. Bed sharing among siblings who have their own individual beds is only an issue if it is a habit that one of them objects to or, in your view, is related to problematic daytime behavior, including violating their siblings' space or rights in other ways, such as taking toys rather than asking permission, constant bickering, or hitting.

Breaking the co-sleeping habit when siblings co-sleep is based on the same principles as breaking the co-sleeping habit between parent and child. Use the age-appropriate procedures provided in Chapters 6 through 8, tailoring the specifics to the situation.

When Your Child Co-Sleeps with Your Former Spouse or Extended Family

You have probably tried to address this issue without success. As much as you might want to, or think it is best, you cannot control the actions of adults outside of your household.

If you and your child's other parent are not together, it's likely that you didn't agree on issues when you were together. You probably didn't agree with some of your parents' opinions and actions when you were younger living in their household. So you may not get their cooperation on the co-sleeping issue either.

The important thing is not to alienate the other adults whom your children love. Even if you are right about an issue, as long as your children are safe spending overnights with their other parent or their grandparents, you have to live with the fact that the rules and philosophies in their homes will not always be the same as yours.

If your child says to you, "But grandma lets me sleep in her bed," or "Dad lies down with me until I fall asleep. It's not fair that you don't," gently tell your child that the rules are different in different homes. Give examples of other ways that you know of that the rules are different in the different homes.

Even if the co-sleeping habit in the other households makes your task of breaking the co-sleeping habit more difficult, do your best not to place blame out loud or in your self-talk. Just stay focused on what you can control and on being the best parent you can be in your domain.

Advice for Parents with Visitation

If you are a parent who only gets to spend time with your child on a weekend, or another part-time arrangement, co-sleeping can be tempting. It may seem like a logical way to spend more time with your child. But if you engage in the co-sleeping habit with a child toddler-aged and up, you may be making the transition between households more difficult for your child. You may also be sending a message that you don't cope well in your child's absence.

Maintaining good boundaries and teaching your child how to self-comfort at bedtime are just as much an obligation for you as for the parent your child lives with the rest of the time. You are just as much of a parent, even if you see your child less frequently than you would like.

During your visitation time, your children need you to be a calm, assertive leader and role model, not someone who clings to them desperately throughout the night.

When you don't see your children every day, you can still maintain a strong attachment. Show an interest in their lives, their opinions, and their feelings. Keep up with what is happening at school, in their extracurricular activities, and with their friendships. Involve them in preparing meals with you and other activities that give them a sense of family at your home.

If Your Child Has ADHD

If your child suffers from attention deficit/hyperactivity disorder (ADHD), then you know it's not just about attention and focus. ADHD is a self-regulation problem that can include sleep disturbance. It's difficult to get your child to go to bed, it's difficult for your child to fall asleep, and then in the morning, you have to pry the child out of bed. You may sometimes wonder what schedule your child would choose to keep if nothing were imposed.

To make matters worse, some children with ADHD have a parent with ADHD who is also unregulated, and maybe a little disorganized. The parent and the child who both have ADHD can get into horrendous struggles at bedtime. If this is your situation, you may be very susceptible for falling into the co-sleeping habit just to avoid the power struggle. Don't do it!

The best way to avoid power struggles with your child at bedtime is to set and maintain a consistent bedtime and routine as well as having the rest of the day structured. The more structure, the better. Children with ADHD thrive on structure. It should start in the morning with the morning routine and then continue after school.

The school day itself is structured by the starting time, the ending time, the teacher, the curriculum, and your child's daily school schedule. Continuing a clear format for your child with ADHD after school will help your child cope with the remaining transitions through bedtime.

When your child gets home, make sure there is a brief time for snack and relaxation and that your child knows how long he or she has. Then, before your child gets too distracted, or any medication he is on wears off, set the child up for doing homework, preferably in the same uncluttered location every day. Dinner should follow, with your child doing a helpful chore. Then, homework that remains should be completed. At this point, for elementary school children, there might be some time left for physical activity before wind-down time.

If your child attends an after-school program and gets home later, you can still provide structure, but getting everything accomplished in a nonrushed fashion will be more challenging.

Remember not to sacrifice winding down and the set bedtime routine.

If you stay calm, you will increase the likelihood of your child with ADHD staying calm as the evening progresses. Use the age-appropriate plan provided in Chapters 6 through 8. Many children with ADHD respond favorably to relaxation techniques.

When Your Child Is Ill

Everyone gets sick from time to time. If you had been entrenched in the co-sleeping habit with your child and have successfully broken that habit, keep in mind that you want to do everything you can to maintain your child's ability to sleep independently. Giving in to co-sleeping when your child doesn't feel well is unnecessary and can make it harder for your child to go back to independent sleep when the illness is over.

If you are worried about your child who is ill and you think your child might need you in the middle of the night and be unable to summon you, then you can set up a temporary bed—cot or sleeping bag—for yourself in your child's room during that period of time. Let your child know that you are staying because of the illness and that you will be sleeping in your own space in the child's room. When your child is better, put away the cot or sleeping bag so that the sight of them doesn't trigger your child to ask you to continue sleeping in the room.

When You Go on a Family Trip

Once you break the co-sleeping habit, you and your child are in recovery. What this means is that any co-sleeping can easily bring you back to square one. This includes family trips and vacations. If you are sharing a hotel or motel room with your child on a trip, book a room that has a bed for your child, have a rollaway bed provided, or bring something for your child to sleep in or on. If you have finally achieved independent sleep after breaking the co-sleeping habit with your child, saying to yourself, "It won't hurt, just this one time" is about as sensible as giving a recovering alcoholic a glass of champagne on New Year's Eve.

Part III

A Closer Look at Families in the Co-Sleeping Habit

This part of the book tells the stories of "families" in which parents and children are in the co-sleeping habit. Each family is really a blend of lots of families with names and details changed. Although the co-sleeping habit takes on different forms and emerges from different circumstance in the families described, the end result is the same—unhappy parents and insecure children.

The stories will illustrate how each type of co-sleeping habit described is linked to children's behavior problems during the day and how establishing boundaries at bedtime helped these children and parents function better night and day.

CHAPTER 10

Tucking In That Never Ends

Tucking in a child is a normal, healthy ritual. It is supposed to be a special, quiet time when you and your child reaffirm your bond. It is a time when you help prepare your child for sleep. It is supposed to be a loving transition for your child from daytime to sleep time. It can be as simple as a kiss on the forehead, or it can be longer and include a bedtime story or quiet conversation.

Of course, tucking-in behavior changes over time. But there is no age limit. It's okay if you tuck in a preteen or teenager (if they want you to). With younger children, you might read a story and make sure they have their favorite stuffed animal and a glass of water so that it is not requested later. With older children, a reassuring smile and brief conversation may be enough. Some children are happy with one parent doing the tucking in and the other parent saying a brief goodnight. In some families, both parents participate at the same time. Whatever the age of your child or your style of tucking in, keep in mind that it is a process that is supposed to end with your leaving the room and your child staying in bed and eventually falling asleep—without you.

When your child doesn't "allow" you to leave the room after being tucked in, your child may not allow you to leave him or her anywhere, including school. This is what happened in the case of Audrey.

The Story of Audrey, Age Five, and Her Parents

Audrey was a five-year-old kindergarten student who reached her developmental milestones on time and had nothing significant in her health history. Audrey's parents had been married two years before conceiving Audrey and were delighted to begin their family.

When family counseling began, Audrey's parents explained that everything was fine until kindergarten started. Actually, the problem began earlier in Audrey's development due to a misunderstanding about her needs at bedtime, which led to daytime fears, an imbalance in the family, and marital issues. Let's start with the school avoidance, and as the story unravels you will see the far-reaching negative impact of the co-sleeping habit in this family.

School Avoidance

Audrey resisted going to school from the start. Although Audrey knew how to dress herself and did so willingly on the weekends, she refused to get dressed for school. She was like a dead weight when her mother struggled to dress her. Pleading with Audrey and threats of consequences made no difference.

Once dressed, she wouldn't eat breakfast and had to be carried to the car, squirming as she got fastened into her car seat. She promptly fell asleep, or appeared to do so, when the engine got going. Upon arriving at school, Audrey would act as though she could not be awakened. When that struggle ended, she would whine and hold on to the car seat, looking terrified about leaving the car to go into the school building. She would say, "I don't want to go," or "My belly hurts."

At first, her mother thought that the teacher was at fault. But after getting to know the teacher, her mom found her to be a kind, nurturing woman. The teacher reassured Audrey's mother that some five-year-olds still have a little separation anxiety and that Audrey would be fine once she got involved in the classroom.

When her mother accompanied her to the kindergarten classroom, Audrey would scream and cling to her. It was hard for Audrey's mother to leave, but after a while she would leave because she knew there was no real threat to Audrey at school. A few minutes after her mother left, Audrey settled down. Sometimes, though, Audrey's mother would come early to take her home. Audrey typically chattered happily in the car all the way home, talking about all the fun things she did at school that day.

Six months into kindergarten, Audrey still refused to leave her mother's car to enter the school building in the morning. Her mother would bring her in with Audrey protesting all along the way. Sometimes, about half way through the school day, Audrey's mother would get a call from the school nurse that Audrey wasn't feeling well and that she should pick her up. Many trips to the pediatrician showed that nothing physical was wrong.

When Audrey's mother asked the pediatrician why her daughter resisted school, the doctor suggested she was an anxious child who might be suffering from a school phobia and that she needed counseling. What the pediatrician didn't know was that it was Audrey's mom who had no idea how to separate from the child, not only during the day, but also at night.

Tucking In Had No Ending

In the same manner that Audrey resisted getting ready for school in the morning, she was uncooperative and whiny as soon as she sensed that bedtime was near. She wouldn't budge when it was time to get ready for bed. Her mom pleaded with her, then bathed her, brushed her teeth for her, helped her into her pajamas, and then started the tucking-in process. Audrey's dad said goodnight to Audrey when she got her goodnight kiss from him in the family room before the bedtime routine began.

Her mom made sure that every stuffed animal that Audrey wanted was in its place and that her baby blankets were folded the way Audrey insisted they needed to be folded. Audrey usually had to go back to the bathroom again and yelled for more help from mom. When Audrey and her mother returned to Audrey's bedroom, the stuffed animals and blankets had to be arranged all over again.

Then, Mom would lie down in Audrey's bed with her and read her daughter a story. Sometimes it took Audrey a long time to choose the story she wanted. She always asked for another story. When her mom tried to set a limit and said, "Just one more," Audrey would agree, but then back out of the deal and insist on another story. They laughed together about how Audrey always backed out of deals, and then her mom would read another story.

One Hour and Counting

Around this time—about an hour after the tucking in had started—dad would stick in his head to say goodnight again to Audrey. He often asked his wife if she would be done soon, and she would tell him she'd be there in just a few minutes. Time would pass.

Audrey's father used to go to bed and wait for his wife, but he began to realize that she would never get there. So he would go into the den and do paperwork. He used to come back to Audrey's room to get his wife, but he learned that he'd either be accused of not letting the child fall asleep or he'd find his wife asleep. So he didn't bother any more. He became the odd man out.

Interrupting During the Day

Because of the lack of adult time in the evening, Audrey's father wanted to spend more adult time during the day with just his wife, but Audrey just wouldn't allow this. She constantly interrupted her parents' conversations and would throw a fit when they tried to engage in any activity that didn't involve her. She didn't even let them have a conversation at the dinner table without interrupting them. Audrey's mother thought that her daughter should be allowed to express herself whenever she wanted to.

Separation Anxiety

Audrey's parents never left her with a babysitter to go out on their own because the child cried inconsolably as soon as she saw them getting ready. They couldn't stand seeing her so upset and felt that they couldn't enjoy their evening out while she was in such a state.

By giving in to Audrey's insistence at bedtime that she could not leave the room, Audrey's mom was giving Audrey the message that she couldn't function anywhere—and didn't have to— without her mom by her side. Audrey's parents didn't see the connection.

The Parents Felt Helpless

Audrey's parents tried to reason with her, console her, bribe her, and punish her by withdrawing privileges, including watching cartoons. Nothing worked. They hoped that she would outgrow her fears as she got older. They felt helpless and just gave in to her. They had no idea how to become the leaders of the family.

How Did the Problem Start?

The funny thing is that when Audrey was a baby, she slept well—all by herself—in her crib. One of her parents would put her down, and after a few minutes she would be asleep. It was easy to comfort her when she would awaken in the middle of the night. The trouble began in the transition from the crib to the toddler bed.

Audrey's parents bought her a toddler bed when she was about two and a half. Rather than preparing her, they took down the crib and assembled the bed as a surprise. When Audrey saw the bed, she took a step back. That night, she refused to get in it unless her mother got in it with her. Then, when her mother attempted to get out of the toddler bed, Audrey protested with tears, begging and holding on tightly to her mother's arm. So her mother stayed, and stayed, and stayed.

Audrey's mother didn't know that Audrey had a capacity to comfort herself and didn't realize that she could teach her daughter coping skills.

Co-Sleeping Became More Entrenched

After about a year of sharing the toddler bed with Audrey, her mom found herself too cramped to sleep with Audrey every night. After failed attempts to go back to sleeping in her marital bed, Audrey's mom bought the child a double bed so that she and her daughter could co-sleep more comfortably. Audrey's dad protested this decision, but Audrey's cries were louder than his.

The summer before Audrey entered kindergarten, Audrey's dad gave her mom an ultimatum. Audrey's mom had to decide whether she wanted her sleeping partner to be her husband or her daughter. Although Audrey's mom valued her marriage, she felt that her husband placed her in a bind. But a part of her was coming to realize that it might be best for Audrey to learn to sleep by herself like a big girl.

A few nights before kindergarten started, Audrey's parents sprung the plan on her. Mom started out in the child's bed and then left for the marital bed. Audrey's dad had lit a few candles, hoping to celebrate the first night they would be together overnight in years. Audrey let her mother leave the bed after a goodnight kiss. But just as her mom entered her own room, Audrey had a full-blown tantrum. So the sleeping arrangement continued.

Mom and Dad Saw It Differently

Neither one of these parents had a clue that the sleeping arrangement in their household was at the heart of Audrey's controlling the family during the day.

Audrey's dad just wanted his wife back. He knew his daughter had a lot of anxiety, but he didn't know why. Mom felt so guilty when Audrey became upset that she kept on reinforcing the clingy, controlling behavior without even realizing it.

Audrey's mom would get angry with her husband when he suggested that maybe Audrey was stronger than she seemed. It wasn't until counseling was underway that Audrey's mother realized the toll the co-sleeping habit took on her marriage.

They Made the Nighttime-Daytime Connection

Through parent counseling, these parents learned how to work together to become the leaders of the family. Audrey's mom realized that she was making Audrey overly dependent on her at bedtime and was also rewarding Audrey's school avoidance. She also realized that her sleeping in Audrey's bed made her husband feel rejected.

Both mother and father helped Audrey cope with going to bed and sleeping independently. They changed the bedtime routine such that Audrey felt success as she engaged in more activities with less help, including brushing her own teeth, getting a cup of water, and even spending some time in the bathtub on her own. Audrey felt more secure as her behavior became more age appropriate. With the support and encouragement from both her parents, Audrey learned to sleep without her mom. Her parents had more private time together and the family became balanced.

When the co-sleeping habit was changed into independent sleep for Audrey, she separated without a problem for school and began to take pride in being a big girl. Audrey became a much happier child. She made friends at school. She actually enjoyed it when her parents went out to dinner occasionally without her because her teenage babysitter was a lot of fun.

Tips for Tucking In

- Keep it structured and time limited.
- Make sure your child has everything he or she needs—in advance.
- Tuck in early enough so that you have time for yourself afterward.
- Provide comfort tools that are age-appropriate, such as stuffed animals or a nightlight.
- Don't lie down with your child no matter how tempting.
- Deal with your children's protests in a calm, assertive manner.
- Reassure your children you will be available.
- Be clear that it is up to them to fall asleep.

CHAPTER 11

The Middle-of-the-Night Wake-Up Call

You work hard during the day and deserve a good, uninterrupted night's sleep. And so do your children. If your child is a toddler or older and wakes you or your partner up more than once in a while, you need to correct this behavior.

Some kids call out from their room. Others come right into your room to get you. It might be at midnight or 2 A.M. or 3 A.M. No matter what the time, you were sound asleep, and now you're not. Or because you begin to expect it, you can't fall asleep.

Do you get out of your warm bed to "save" your child? If you do, you're not the only one. Thousands of parents are put to the test. In fact, some parents of teenagers—age sixteen, seventeen, and eighteen—still get out of bed and tuck in their kids again in the middle of the night—five or six nights a week!

The Story of Sam, Age Nine, and His Parents

Sam was a nine-year-old who functioned well both at home and at school until his baby sister was born two years ago. Although Sam was fortunate to have supportive parents and grandparents, he had difficulty adapting to no longer being an only child and to getting less attention from his mother. Sam's behavior regressed more and more because of the co-sleeping habit that his parents allowed to develop.

School Issues

Sam's third-grade teacher told his parents at a school conference that the child might benefit from counseling or a psychological evaluation. The teacher shared her concern that Sam often put his head down on his desk and had to have his name called several times before he would sit up. At recess, he played with the other children, but he took his time getting back to the classroom. He wasn't hyperactive, but he seemed to be in a world of his own. The teacher suspected Sam had attention deficit disorder (ADD).

Sam's father and mother were both concerned. In the spring of that school year, when Sam's behavior was not improving, his mother made the call to the therapist and explained on the phone that Sam was not attentive in school. Although he wasn't disruptive in class, he didn't follow directions and avoided doing his work. At this point, he was also making frequent requests to go the bathroom and to the nurse's office where he would lie down. He showed little interest in going back to class.

In previous school years, he concentrated well and seemed enthusiastic about school. His past teachers never mentioned a problem with focus, but Sam's mother wondered if maybe the problem was showing up now because the work was now more challenging.

Sam's mom was worried that Sam would fall behind academically and would never make it to college. The therapist requested that both parents come to the initial session. Even though the call came in from Sam's mom, Sam's dad went to the first counseling session by himself.

Sam's dad reported that he and his wife planned Sam's conception and were thrilled when he was born. He was a full-term, healthy baby. Sam had the attention of both his parents, who ran a business from home. Sam's maternal grandparents, who lived nearby, doted on him.

This Child Regressed after the Birth of the Baby

Until the birth of his sister two years ago, Sam had been an outgoing child. He joked around like one of the adults. He had always looked forward to going to his grandparents' house and helping his grandpa in his wood shop. Sam would ask to be taken to the playground every day, even if it was raining. He would run around for hours at the playground and had no trouble making new friends. He cooperated when playtime was over.

Sam also did well in school. His kindergarten and first-grade teachers marveled at how easily he picked up the basic skills of reading, writing, and math. In second grade, he played soccer.

When Sam was no longer an only child, he changed. Even though Sam's parents prepared him for his sister's arrival, he became sullen and unmotivated from the day she was brought home.

A year later, at age eight, instead of adjusting to being a big brother, Sam's attitude was even worse. He showed no interest in sharing in the joy of her accomplishments when she began to walk and say words, he refused to help blow out the candle on the baby's first birthday, and he didn't want to play with her.

Sam began to watch a lot of TV. His grades and behavior in school went downhill. His dad would offer to kick the soccer ball around with Sam, and would be met with "No, thank you." Sam would do his homework only if someone stood over him. When he went over to his grandparents' house, he was polite but lost his interest in spending time in the wood shop.

By age nine, Sam hardly ever joked around any more. He just wasn't the same child. It didn't sound like ADD because Sam's focus had been fine during his early school years. He had learned the basics and did not display impulsivity or hyperactivity.

The birth of Sam's sister appeared to be a factor in his emotional and behavioral slump. But why wasn't he adapting?

The Bedtime Routine Fell Apart

Although Sam's parents did a good job preparing him for his sister's birth by involving him in the sibling class at the hospital and giving him hugs and attention after she was born, they were in the dark about how to parent him effectively at night.

Within a few days of the baby's birth, Sam began to resist going to bed. Up to this time, he never put up much of a fuss about bedtime. His mom would help him get ready and tuck him in with a bedtime story and a kiss. His dad would come in later to give Sam a goodnight kiss, and that was that, unless Sam didn't feel well.

Because his mom now had to tend to the baby, his dad became more involved with Sam's bedtime routine. The balance of the family had changed. It was his mom with baby and his dad with Sam.

Sam began to whine at bedtime and took longer to get ready. His dad reacted by spending more time with him at night, which they both enjoyed. They watched TV together in the den and lost track of Sam's bedtime. But the time and reassurance Sam needed after the birth of his sister seemed reasonable.

Even though Sam took an extra hour or so to get to bed and fall asleep, the slightly drawn-out bedtime routine wasn't the real culprit. The serious trouble began in the middle of the night. Sam didn't stay asleep. And the co-sleeping habit between Sam and his father began.

Two Years into the Co-Sleeping Habit

For two years, Sam awakened almost every night and called out from his bed to his parents. At the start of the habit, Sam would call out for his mother. "Mom, I had a bad dream" or "Mom, I don't feel good." When she called out to him that he should try to get back to sleep, he would cry.

Sam's mom was tired from tending to the baby's middle-of-the-night cries, so her husband would go to Sam to comfort him. But brief reassurances and hugs were not enough to comfort Sam. He would beg his father to stay with him in his bed, and his father gave in.

It wasn't long before Sam called out only to his father. "Dad, I had a bad dream and I can't get back to sleep." "Dad, I have another belly ache."

When the pattern first started, Sam's dad would try after a while to go back to his own bed. But Sam, who appeared to be sleeping, would bolt up and protest, resulting in his dad spending the night, night after night. His dad felt Sam needed him to stay and didn't know what else to do.

Even though Sam's dad didn't start out in his son's bed, he ended up there and didn't leave for two years. Instead of making Sam feel secure, this dad's well-intentioned behavior triggered even more insecurity in his nine-year-old son.

These Parents Finally Saw the Connection

Sam's father, though well intentioned, was engaging in reactive co-sleeping, which exaggerated the imbalance that evolved after the birth of the baby. Sam's parents learned how to work together to re-establish the secure attachment that they had fostered with Sam before the birth of the baby.

Both parents attended the second counseling session. The therapist suggested that before sending Sam for testing for possible ADD, some changes in the family's routines might be helpful, starting with nighttime parenting. Sam's parents began to realize that the co-sleeping habit, instead of helping Sam feel more secure, was feeding into his insecurities about his place in the family. Sam's behavior was regressive and was being reinforced. On top of that, there was an imbalance in the family that needed to be changed so that Sam could spend some time with his mom, which he missed, and his dad could have some more time with the younger child. Also, Sam's mom and dad could have some time together with neither child.

Testing for ADD became unnecessary. Once the connections in the family became balanced, Sam's behavior in school improved. He was less preoccupied and more focused. He also regained interest in spending time with his grandparents. He even began to enjoy his little sister's antics and accomplishments.

Tips for the Middle-of-the-Night Wake-Up Call

- Do not reward nighttime interrupting.
- Make a commitment to notice if your child enters your bed.
- Remember that changing this habit will lead to less daytime interrupting.
- Remind your child before bed that you will not co-sleep in reaction to calling out.
- Remind your child before bed to value your privacy.
- Support your spouse in breaking this reactive co-sleeping habit.
- Do not play musical beds.
- Make sure your child has everything he or she needs at bedtime.
- Remind yourself not to reward manipulative behavior.
- Make a plan to spend more time with your children during the day.

CHAPTER 12

Your Child Starts Off in
Your Bed and Never Leaves

What could possibly be wrong with your children watching TV in your bed at night? What's wrong with your children snuggling up with you in your bed before they go to sleep? Nothing, really—unless they never leave.

It seems so cozy, so close knit and warm. There you are with your child, or there you are with a bunch of kids—all under the covers, ending the day together in the big bed, and then starting the next day after having had no separation at all.

If it's not a conscious decision on your part to co-sleep but just kind of turns out that way, night after night, then it's a bad idea.

The Story of Lilly, Age Four, and Her Parents

Lilly, a verbal, adorable four-year-old, controlled her parents. Her mother sounded tearful on the phone as she explained to the therapist that when Lilly doesn't get her way, everyone around her suffers. So "we give in."

When the therapist requested that both parents come to the first session without their child, Lilly's mom explained that Lilly wouldn't like it if her parents saw the therapist behind her back. That was all the more reason for them to come without her the first time. These parents lived in fear of their four-year-old child's reactions to their decisions.

Lilly's parents were both professionals in their early thirties, her dad a dermatologist and her mom a computer programmer. Lilly's grandmother frequently picked up Lilly from preschool and stayed with her until one of her parents got home. Lilly cooperated with her grandma who idolized the child and let her eat and do anything she wanted.

The Child Was in Charge of the Family

Both parents were worried about Lilly because she threw tantrums. When she had a tantrum in public, they didn't know what to do and worried what other people would think about them as parents.

Lilly was in so much control of the family that she would dictate which one of her parents should drive the car, and they would comply. They explained at the first session that the family would get into the car to go out to dinner and Lilly would say, "I want mom to drive" if her dad was entering the driver's side, or she would say, "I want dad to drive" if her mom was going to drive. If they didn't switch, she would break free of her car seat, scream, stomp her feet, and make it impossible to leave. So they would give in.

One night, the three of them were going out to dinner. Lilly said, "I want Chinese food." Her dad told her that he had Chinese food for lunch, so tonight they were having Italian. Lilly threw a fit. She thrashed around on the floor of the family room and screamed that she hated Italian food. When her parents asked her to calm down, she told them, "I hate you," ran into the bathroom, and locked the door. Her mother resolved the conflict by telling Lilly through the bathroom door that they would all go to a diner where everyone could get what they wanted. Lilly came out with a smile. After all the fuss about not wanting to go to an Italian restaurant, Lilly ordered eggplant Parmesan and spaghetti at the diner and relished every bite. Her mom was horrified and couldn't eat.

Lilly's parents couldn't get her to comply with simple requests. She would act as though she didn't hear when asked to put her toys away or to come to the table. When asked in a louder voice, Lilly would cry and tell her parents they were being mean to her. She would tell her grandmother the next time she saw her how mean her parents were to her. Then, her grandmother would call Lilly's dad and scold him for being too demanding. "She's just a little girl."

Lilly's mom revealed to the therapist in a whisper that she feared the child had no conscience. Lilly's dad told his wife she was being ridiculous and that the child was simply spoiled.

They Tried Everything, or Did They?

Lilly's parents said they had tried everything to change her behavior. Her mom had given her timeouts (four minutes for each year of age, as the pediatrician recommended), had sent her to her room, and had removed her toys. Her dad had tried reasoning with her and asking her why she misbehaved. They tried spending more time with her doing things she liked, and tried the reverse—insisted that she fit in with their agenda. Nothing worked. Yelling and confrontations made things worse.

The Path of Least Resistance at Bedtime

At night, Lilly became a loving child. She liked to sit on her mom's lap in the evening. She played board games with her dad and was a good sport even when she lost. She seemed to comply with requests better late in the evening than during the day. She willingly did a prebedtime routine. She put on her pajamas when asked to, brushed her own teeth like a big girl, and even got herself a drink of water. So when Lilly wanted to hang out on her parents' bed at night and watch TV with them, or just be with them for a while in their big bed before she went into her own room, they were thrilled to have this peaceful, loving time with their daughter. Why rock the boat when she was being so good?

At first, after getting into her pajamas, she would stay with her parents on top of their bed between a half hour to an hour, and then let one of them tuck her into her own bed. But as time went on, she stayed longer and got under the covers. It became harder and harder to get her to leave without triggering her vengeful side. As soon as either of them got up to escort her to her own bed, she displayed the early signs of a tantrum. They felt so bad when she was mean or cold to them that they would do just about anything to appease her. And thus, the co-sleeping habit took hold. Lilly's parents engaged in reactive parenting during the day and were reactive co-sleepers at night.

Once the habit took hold, the family engaged in a dynamic in which they all pretended that Lilly would be staying for only a short while in the big bed. They played a game about Lilly going to her own bed. They all really knew at this point that Lilly would be staying for the night, every night. Her mom would say, "Okay, you can stay a few more minutes," or her dad would say, "I'll go and tuck you in soon," and then they would sleep with Lilly between them until morning.

Once it was morning, the power struggles began again. As cooperative as Lilly had been in doing her bedtime routine the night before, she was equally uncooperative getting ready for the day.

These Parent Felt Helpless

The sleeping arrangement undermined these parents' authority. Lilly held her parents in bondage, not only during the day, but also all night, and they let it happen. Rather than the parents being the leaders of the family, their four-year-old was in control of the family and the household, day and night.

During the day, Lilly's parents did whatever she wanted, no matter how unreasonably she behaved, because they were afraid of her and were overly affected by her behavior. They reinforced her bad behavior and taught her how to manipulate rather than healthy coping skills.

During the night, they sacrificed their own privacy to maintain peace. They had no time alone for intimate talk or anything else. They were also so grateful for the loving child Lilly turned into at night, that they didn't want to let go of that. They let the co-sleeping habit develop through a process of emotional reasoning. They didn't realize that they could help her be a loving child during the day, as well, and that they didn't have to sacrifice their adult relationship to achieve this goal.

The Parents Restored the Balance

Through parent counseling, Lilly's parents developed insight into the role reversal that had taken place in their family. They realized that Lilly's being in charge was not good for her self-image and was not good for their family. The tantrums were just one symptom out of a larger dynamic of control and balance issues.

Even though Lilly's parents thought they had tried everything, they were just putting out fires, by addressing each of Lilly's outbursts, unsuccessfully. What they had not tried was restoring balance at bedtime.

Lilly had slept independently as a younger child, so her parents knew she could do it. They made a plan and let Lilly know in advance what to expect. They told her that it was time for her to sleep in her own room again and that they would be nearby if she needed them. The hardest part for these parents was the follow through, but they were successful because they knew that their daughter needed to learn self-control and how to let go of controlling other people. They also wanted some adult time at night and realized there was no reason to feel guilty about that.

They also made the decision to enroll Lilly in preschool. Even though Lilly's grandmother was available, they felt that Lilly would benefit from the structure of the preschool program. Lilly thrived in preschool. It gave her purpose, and she learned how to compromise. Lilly adapted to listening to her teacher, and she quickly made friends. Her tantrums subsided.

Lilly's parents had learned how to make the changes necessary for them to become the leaders of the family. It started with breaking the co-sleeping habit.

Tips for Parents When the Child Never Leaves Your Bed

- Have the bedtime routine in the child's room—not in your bedroom.
- Cuddle with your children on the sofa—then tuck them into their beds.
- Say "No" and stick to it if your child asks or demands to spend time before bed in your bed.
- Make sure you're not tricking yourself into the co-sleeping habit by telling yourself that you will tuck the child into his or her bed later—and then you don't do it.
- Do not let this co-sleeping habit continue if your child is comforting you.
- Keep the family bed if it is a conscious parenting plan that is agreed upon between you and your spouse and if your child seems to be benefiting from the co-sleeping arrangement.

CHAPTER 13

Sneaking into Your Bed "Unnoticed"

Parents have often told me that their children sneak into their room in the middle of the night unnoticed. Some parents find their children in bed next to them in the morning and either don't remember their coming in or were just too tired to put them back to bed.

Does this happen to you?

The Story of Benjamin, Age Seven, and His Parents

Benjamin, age seven, was talkative with his mom, but quiet with everyone else. He had no difficulty separating from her when he went to school, but once there, he stayed apart from his classmates during recess and hung out quietly near the teachers. He rarely raised his hand in class even when he knew the answer. He didn't want to participate in team sports. He didn't know the rules of the games, was afraid to look awkward in front of his peers, and said he didn't care anyway.

Benjamin's mom was worried that he would grow up to be lonely if she was his only source of social enjoyment. So she called a therapist. The therapist recommended that she come in with her husband for the first appointment. Benjamin's mother hesitated and then explained that her husband thought she was overreacting and that he didn't believe in therapy. She didn't want him to know she made the call. She just wanted some advice. She came to the first session by herself.

A Little Family History

Benjamin's mom was age fifty and his father was forty-nine. She and her husband were married for twenty-eight years. She was a retired attorney and her husband worked for the state. They had two daughters, ages twenty-seven and twenty-five, who lived about 500 miles away. The older daughter was disabled and lived with her sister and brother-in-law who were high school teachers.

By the time Benjamin was age two, his sisters had moved out of the house. Over the next five years, he saw them and his brother-in-law almost every Christmas and one other time when he was five.

He Was a Miracle Baby

Benjamin was a surprise. His mother explained that she and her husband felt blessed to have another chance at being parents later in life. Benjamin's mother had an amniocentesis to make sure the baby was okay, and he was. He weighed ten pounds, six ounces at birth. He walked and talked early. Wherever she and her husband went with their son, people assumed he was their grandson, but they didn't care. He was their little miracle.

They never had the closeness with their daughters that they felt with their son. Their firstborn daughter, Joanie, had autism. As much as they loved her, her disability did not allow for the depth of emotional bond that they craved. Their second born daughter, Melinda, was fine, but felt neglected because of all the attention and care needed by her older sister. Melinda resolved her dilemma by becoming an overachiever and caregiver for her older sister. It was Melinda's decision to have Joanie live with her and her husband, Albert, who was also a nurturer. When Benjamin was born, the parents felt that their joy had to be subdued in front of Melinda, whom they assumed must be jealous but hiding it well.

Mom Made Her Son Helpless—But She Didn't Realize It

Benjamin was a happy baby who ate and slept on a regular schedule. His mom stopped working a few years after he was born so that she could be home with him full time. She noticed that he was shy starting at about age three, but thought nothing of it. However, when at age four he still hid behind her when she would run into a friend at the market and he wouldn't play with the neighborhood kids, she started to worry. When Benjamin's mother expressed her concern to her husband, he pooh-poohed her and said that she was still a worrywart because of Joanie, that there was nothing wrong with Ben.

In counseling, when talking about the difference in points of view between her and her husband, she began to cry. She felt that their daughter Joanie had Melinda, but who would take care of Benjamin after she and her husband were gone?

When asked to describe Benjamin's daily routine, it came to light that Benjamin's mother was treating him as though he were disabled, both during the day and during the night. At age seven, she treated him more like age three. She selected his clothes for him, helped him get dressed, and aided him in just about every task of daily living. She didn't think he could put together a bowl of cereal and milk. She wouldn't let him spread peanut butter on a cracker with a butter knife for fear he would cut himself. She sat next to him at the dining room table every day after school and helped him with his homework, whether he needed help or not.

At bedtime, she and her husband tucked the boy in and said goodnight. He fell asleep pretty quickly. His mom checked on him about every ten minutes for over a two-hour period before she went to bed to make sure he was alright.

In the morning, every morning, she and her husband would find the boy in their bed, sometimes at the bottom scrunched between their feet and the footboard, sometimes next to her, and sometimes between them. She told the therapist that she had no idea when he snuck in, but it was sometime during the night. She didn't think it was a problem. In fact, she took it as a positive sign that Benjamin needed her as much during the night as he did during the day. Benjamin's mother said that she and her husband never discussed the sleep pattern with Benjamin because they didn't want him to feel rejected or alone.

This pattern had been occurring almost every night for four years, since Benjamin was age three. Although this wasn't the issue that brought this family into counseling, this reactive, unplanned co-sleeping habit came to light as part of the intake process. Benjamin's parents' facing the habit and what maintained it were key factors in helping Benjamin and his family.

The Family Was Out of Balance

Both of Benjamin's parents attended the next session. It turned out that Benjamin's father was not only aware that his son snuck into his bed but felt fulfilled by it. Benjamin's father was happy that his son snuck into their bed in the night because he felt it was the only time he could get close to his son. During the day, his wife smothered Ben and was so possessive of the boy that he felt he had no choice but to take a back seat.

Benjamin's father felt alone when his daughters left. He viewed Benjamin's birth as an opportunity to be close to someone. But as it turned out, now he was more alone than ever. He loved the time that he spent in proximity to his son during the night. In fact, he admitted to sometimes keeping himself awake, waiting for his arrival.

Based on the parents' input, it appeared that Benjamin's motives for sneaking into their bed at night were complex and that the child might have been having difficulty distinguishing their needs from his own. He had difficulty separating his identity from his mother's, and he had a need for closeness with his father that he didn't know how to express during the day. Thus, rather than being based on attachment, the co-sleeping was based on enmeshment.

Their enmeshed sleep pattern indicated that Benjamin's parents were in the dark about meeting and balancing their child's needs, their own, and each other's for a long time. It was a reactive parenting style that put a Band-Aid on a problem, and under the Band-Aid was a wound that could not heal until it was uncovered and dealt with.

Creating a Healthy Balance

The enmeshed sleep pattern was one of many symptoms of misalignment in Benjamin's family. This family needed to learn how to relate to each other during the day in ways that would improve the communication between the parents, strengthen the bond between Benjamin and his father, and help Benjamin feel like a fully functioning seven-year-old.

Changing the enmeshed co-sleeping habit gave Benjamin and his parents the opportunity to live more fully during the day. The parents opened up their communication with each other. They worked as partners to help Benjamin sleep through the night in his own bed.

This process was accompanied by Benjamin's mother learning to let go of some negative thinking habits and old fears, which included equating her nondisabled son with her disabled daughter. Trusting her son to flourish included letting Benjamin's father play a more active role in his son's life during the day. The positive impact of these changes showed up in Benjamin's making a friend, volunteering more in the classroom, and feeling free to give his dad hugs during the day.

Tips for Parents Whose Children Sneak In Unnoticed

- Stop telling yourself and others that you don't notice your child coming into bed.
- If you really don't notice, you must change this. It is a survival tool to notice when another human being enters your bed.
- Do not encourage your children to sneak into each other's beds.
- Do not displace your spouse.
- Escort your child back into his or her bed, no matter how late it is.
- Escort your child back to bed until your child stays there—no matter how many time it takes.
- Do not provide any rewards or conversation when escorting your child back to bed.
- In the morning, praise you child for staying in his or her bed.

CHAPTER 14

The Divorced or Single Parent

Wanting to hold your children close when your world falls apart is a natural instinct. It's not always easy to separate your needs from theirs. But you should.

What your children need from you during the trauma of divorce is reassurance that you will be there for them—but not in the same bed all night long every night.

The story of Anthony and Cassie, brother and sister, will give you a flavor of how easy it is to get into this type of co-sleeping habit and why sleeping with your children when you are lonely is a mistake.

The Story of Anthony, Age Eight, Cassie, Age Six, and Their Parents

Sally and George are divorced and have two children, Anthony, age eight, and Cassie, age six. This family was referred to a psychologist for an evaluation by a family court judge because the children were not available for the court-ordered overnight visitation with the father.

The Children Stopped Going on Overnight Visitation

The father's view was that their mother was withholding them and in violation of their custody agreement. The mother's view was that the children didn't want to go and she wasn't going to force them to go against their wishes. The question to be answered for the court was whether there was any reason that it would not be in the children's best interest to have overnight visitation with their father as stated in the parents' agreement.

Was there a real threat or danger to Anthony or Cassie at their dad's house? If not, what were these children avoiding at dad's house? What were they getting out of staying with their mom instead of going on the overnights with their dad?

The Family

Sally and George were married for a year before they had their first child, Anthony. Two years later, Cassie was born. George owned and managed a restaurant and worked long hours. Sally was a housewife and the primary caregiver of the children. She took excellent care of the home and was an involved parent. George played with the children in the evenings if he came home early enough, and he spent Sundays with them. Unfortunately, the restaurant business meant working many late nights.

When Anthony started kindergarten, the parents arranged for preschool for Cassie. The children made a good adaptation to their school environments. The family looked happy on the outside, but the marriage was troubled.

The End of the Marriage

George and Sally grew distant from each other. They didn't have loud arguments. It was more that their marriage failed to thrive, and then died. They tried a few sessions of marriage counseling, but it seemed like too little too late. The couple decided to separate. About a year later, they had an amicable divorce. They didn't really become friends, but they weren't enemies either. They talked about the children in a civil manner, but as was the case during their marriage, their discussions were not in depth.

Visitation Started Out Okay but Fell Apart

The custody arrangement was that the kids would live primarily with Sally and would see their father every other weekend from Friday night through Sunday after dinner. This was more time than they had ever spent with him before the separation. George hired a manager at the restaurant to free up his time, something he realized he should have done before the marriage went downhill.

At first, when Anthony was six and his sister was four, the children happily saw their father for visitation, including overnights. Although the children were troubled by the divorce, they appeared to be coping reasonably well. However, less than a year later, when George became seriously involved with Helen, a woman he met through a friend on a blind date, the children started resisting staying overnight with their dad.

George swore to Sally that Helen never stayed the night when he had the children, so there was no reason that they should feel uncomfortable being with him. The children admitted to liking Helen, at least a little bit, and confirmed that she was not at their dad's house overnight.

The Children's Behavior Deteriorated

At the same time that the children resisted and eventually refused overnight visits with their dad, other problem behaviors cropped up at their mom's house.

Anthony started to perceive himself as the man of the house at his mom's, but in a distorted way. He would ask her to account for her time, and he intruded on her privacy by going through her desk and dresser drawers. He acted as though he was in charge of her. He wouldn't allow her to date. He was intrusive, and although childlike, he acted as though he became the parent and his mother became his daughter.

At the same time, Cassie became clingy to both her mom and to her brother. She cried when separated from either of them. She followed them around, even into the bathroom.

Cassie started to wet the bed. Her mom explained to the therapist that this behavior was particularly troubling because both she and Anthony had to endure the smell of pee all night. This is how it came to light that they all slept in the same bed.

A Complicated Co-Sleeping Habit

It turned out that the co-sleeping started well before the marital separation. On those nights that George worked late, the children often climbed into bed with their mom. She invited them to stay because snuggling with her children all night made her feel safe. Sometimes they all fell asleep until morning, and sometimes Sally would get up and put them back into their own beds. She resisted putting them into their owns beds more and more, however, because taking this action made her feel like a mean person. She also felt that her children were still her babies and they needed to feel protected and safe by being able to touch her whenever they wanted—just as much as she needed that from them.

After the separation, Sally felt desperately alone. She decided that even if she had to live her life alone, she did not have to be alone through the night. And neither did her babies. They would always be there for her, and she would be there for them. So she made the master bedroom the bedroom that the three of them shared. They all kept their nighttime stuff by the bed, and the children's clothes for the next day were laid out in this room.

Sally thought there was no reason to waste the space that used to be the children's rooms. Because Anthony didn't use his bed any more, it was moved to the basement so that his room could be used as a playroom. Cassie's room became an in-home office. Cassie's bed was still there, but it was covered with stacks of papers.

Although the co-sleeping was a conscious decision on Sally's part, she was co-sleeping with the children for the wrong reasons. She also eliminated each child's personal space.

When Anthony and Cassie first went to their dad's new house for overnights, they slept with him. They expected to, and he was accepting of it. He felt he had so much to make up for because he neglected their emotional needs during the marriage. After the marriage failed, he felt even more guilty.

Then, George began to date Helen. She had young children who slept independently. She told George that his co-sleeping arrangement did not sound beneficial to the children. From what he shared with Helen about the children, she thought they needed more time with him during the day, not during the night. She also didn't see how she and George could plan a future if he continued to co-sleep with his children. She thought that children at that age would benefit from having some privacy as much as he would.

He decided that what Helen said made sense. But he made two mistakes. He didn't discuss the change he was about to make with the children's mother, and he did not prepare the children. He simply stopped allowing them to co-sleep with him or with each other, and he set up the spare room for them with bunk beds as a surprise for their next visit.

He and the children immediately got into power struggles about the sleeping arrangements the first night. When he didn't let them in his bed anymore, they slept together in the bottom bunk. When George insisted to the children that one of them choose the top bunk and the other the bottom, they refused to see him for overnights.

Although George knew what the problem was in a surface way, he did not know how to communicate with his children or their mother about it. He perceived their closeness with their mother as the underlying reason for the children's refusal to continue visitation and failed to recognize the complexity of their feelings when the new sleeping arrangement at his house was sprung on them without warning or discussion.

Ending the Co-Sleeping Habit Ended the Conflict

Each of these parents slept with their children for different reasons. Sally felt alone when George worked late, and even more alone after the separation. She engaged in the co-sleeping habit because she found it comforting. She did not have the insight that the children's daytime behavior—Anthony acting like a parent/dictator and Cassie's bedwetting and clinginess—were a reflection of her own insecurities that manifested themselves in an enmeshed co-sleeping habit.

George tried to compensate for his unavailability during the day by co-sleeping at night. He didn't realize that making a sudden shift wasn't the answer. A change to independent sleep with children who are deeply entrenched in the co-sleeping habit requires sensitivity and planning.

This family's co-sleeping pattern and poor communication about it triggered insecurities and avoidance behaviors in Anthony and Cassie that were at the heart of the problem the court was trying to resolve. Through family counseling, the parents learned better communication tools. Through individual counseling, Sally worked through her insecurities and began to separate her needs from the needs of her children. George became better connected with himself and his children.

It was fortunate for this family that the visitation issue came to a head because resolving it improved the functioning of both of these children and their parents.

Tips for Divorced and Single Parents

- Do not rely on your children for comfort and support.
- Set bedtime boundaries.
- Don't co-sleep with your children in reaction to their feelings of loss.
- Don't co-sleep with your children in reaction to your feelings of loss.
- Separate in your mind their needs from your needs.
- Balance discipline with fun.
- Maintain and build strong friendships.
- Develop your own adult interests and activities.
- Spend more time with your children during the day.
- Let your children see you coping well during the day.
- Support your children's relationships with extended family.
- Support your children's interests and friendships.
- Keep the line of communication open with your children's other parent.

CHAPTER 15

The Ultimate Co-Sleep Imbalance

Are you married or sharing your life with someone? Did you used to share the same bed but now one of you shares a bed with your child or children while your partner sleeps alone—somewhere else in the house? Was this the arrangement that you planned, or has it become a habit that has created imbalance in the family unit? This type of co-sleeping habit is a bad idea, whether your child is a two-year-old, a teen, or in between.

The following story about a middle school student and his parents shows how this imbalance at bedtime can negatively affect everyone in the family.

The Story of Charlie, Age Thirteen, and His Parents

Charlie was referred to counseling by the school principal. She told the parents that if they didn't put him in therapy, he might not be able to stay at the middle school. Now in the eighth grade, counseling had been recommended two years ago when Charlie was in the sixth grade, but his parents did not think it was needed. They thought his behavior would improve with maturity. Since then, he had been suspended twice, and now, Charlie's parents were worried.

This Middle School Student Was a Bully

What concerned the school was that Charlie had become a bully. He intimidated a learning-disabled student and had sexually harassed a classmate in the cafeteria by calling her a name that is a derogatory sexual slur. Charlie didn't deny his behavior, but he didn't feel he did anything wrong. He always had an excuse to justify his actions.

The First Counseling Session

When Charlie's parents came to the first session, they brought Charlie with them, even though they knew it was a parent session and that a meeting with their son was scheduled for two days later. In the waiting room, Charlie's mother stated abruptly that she and Charlie's father had nothing to hide from their son and that they wanted him at the first meeting. When the family entered the therapist's office, which had ample seating, Charlie's dad sat alone on the sofa, which was large enough to accommodate three adults, mom chose an armchair, and Charlie sat on the arm of his mother's chair. Charlie, who was tall for his age and overweight, crowded his petite mother, but she didn't seem to notice.

Mother and Son Were Enmeshed

The therapist asked the family their reasons for coming to counseling. Charlie's mom spoke first and at length. She explained that the school system had it in for her son because he didn't conform to the strict artificial structure imposed on students.

She patted Charlie's back as she explained that her son was frustrated in the school environment. She justified his actions. She stated that when Charlie expressed himself in school, he was not heard and his needs were not met, and that's why he began to express himself more loudly. Although she did not always agree with her son's actions, she felt it was up to the school to provide an atmosphere that would allow him to flourish.

She said the reason she came to the therapy session was because she felt threatened that if she didn't, the school system would discriminate against her son and attempt to send him to a special school for "bad" boys.

Even though the question about why the family was there had been asked of the group, no one else responded after Charlie's mom stopped speaking. It appeared that she had spoken for herself and her son, and Charlie's dad was not accustomed to giving his opinion on family matters. So the therapist asked dad directly why he came.

He responded that he came because his wife told him he had to come. He didn't think that therapy would do them any good. Charlie's father expressed the belief that people are who they are and cannot change. When asked what he thought would happen if his son's behavior didn't change, Charlie's dad responded that he guessed his son would be thrown out of school, which he probably deserved.

Charlie's response to the question of why he came to counseling was, "I don't know."

At that point, the therapist decided to speak with the parents alone to get more background information.

The Problem Started Before Charlie Was Born

Charlie's parents had been married twenty years. His dad, age forty-one, was a successful accountant. His mom, age forty, was a paralegal in a large law firm. Shortly after they were married, they had a baby who died during childbirth from a congenital heart defect. The couple's grief was intense.

About a year later, they decided to take the risk of having another child. But even with fertility medication, they could not conceive. For a long time, their lives revolved around ovulation. Their love life became tense. After seven years of trying, they decided to adopt a child.

Charlie was adopted at birth. His biological mother was a teenager, and his biological father was unknown. Charlie's mom insisted, against all advice, that Charlie should never know that he was adopted. Charlie's father disagreed, but went along with it. He felt that his wife had been through so much that he didn't want to force his opinions on her.

Charlie's parents set up a beautiful nursery for him, fulfilling a dream that they had for many years. Charlie slept well in his crib. Both parents modified their work schedules to spend quality time with their son when he was a baby.

Asthma Led to Co-Sleeping

Around the time Charlie entered preschool, he developed the symptoms of asthma. Sometimes it got so bad that he had to be rushed to the emergency room. He has been on a strict regimen of asthma medication since that time.

Because his parents worried that he might suffer an asthma attack in the middle of the night, they decided that to be on the safe side, their son should sleep with them in their bed.

Dad Became the Odd Man Out

At first, when Charlie was three and four years old, the co-sleeping seemed to be going fine. However, when Charlie entered kindergarten, he had a growth spurt and the bed felt crowded to dad. When Charlie's dad spoke to his wife about Charlie going back to his own bed, she wouldn't hear of it. Even though Charlie's asthma was under control, his mother felt that he could have an attack in the middle of the night, and if he were sleeping alone in his room, she thought he would die and it would be her fault for not being there to save him.

As time went on, Charlie's dad spent less and less time in the family bed and more time on the pullout sofa in the den. By the time Charlie was age six, Charlie routinely co-slept with mom, and dad routinely slept in the den.

Daytime Behavior Problems Developed

Around the same time, Charlie began to gain a lot of weight and developed problems in his peer relationships. When he didn't get his way with other kids, he yelled profanities at them. By first grade, he was invited less often to his friends' houses.

His parents began to get called to school conferences about his behavior. Charlie always minimized his actions. He thought he was the victim. He would beg his mom to bail him out, and she did. Because he didn't give her any trouble, she couldn't understand why the teachers singled out her son.

These Parents Faced Their Fears

In a later session with the parents, which took place while Charlie was in school, Charlie's dad broke down. He told his wife how much he missed her. He reminded her how badly they wanted a child and how he feels left out in the cold and not like a parent or a husband. Eventually, her armor cracked as well. She admitted to her fears about losing Charlie to either his biological mother or to his asthma. She couldn't take it if she lost a second child.

The willingness of these parents to break through their own defenses was the first step toward realigning this family and establishing more balanced connections. Their making a plan to break the co-sleeping habit and work toward normalizing the sleep patterns in their household was the logical next step.

Tips for Parents When One Sleeps with the Child and the Other Parent Sleeps Elsewhere

- Allow yourself to face the imbalance in this family sleep pattern.
- Think about whether you are overinvolved or underinvolved with your child.

- Pinpoint how you think this sleep imbalance affects the family during the day.
- Think about the impact on your marriage.
- Have an ongoing open discussion with your partner without your child present.
- Discuss with your partner how this co-sleeping imbalance got started.
- Discuss with your partner how this sleeping arrangement is affecting your feelings.
- Discuss with your partner your views of the impact on your child.
- Discuss with your partner the steps you can take to create balance for sleeping.
- Discuss with your partner how you can balance your parenting during the day.
- Support each other in spite of the distance this type of co-sleeping habit may have created in your relationship.

Conclusion

Although this book has focused on breaking the co-sleeping habit, it is about much more than that. It is about getting on—and staying on—the path to raising secure children.

By breaking the co-sleeping habit, you as a parent will grow as a leader in your family. You will be better equipped to guide your children on their journey to becoming secure, well functioning adults. By breaking the co-sleeping habit, you will not only accomplish teaching your children to sleep independently (and reclaim your own independent sleep), but you will also show them that you can be loving and consistent at the same time, that you can keep your word and follow through for their best interest, and that you can be relied upon to protect them and keep them safe—even if you are not in their beds.

Projecting strength and leadership as a parent will help your children function better not only at bedtime but also during the day. You will be providing them with a role model that they will be proud to emulate as they develop through adolescence and adulthood.

Co-Sleep Quiz 3

Now that you have read, and perhaps begun to apply, the information in this book, it would be valuable for you to see to what extent you have changed your thinking and goals as a parent. Co-Sleep Quiz 3 is designed to help you evaluate where you stand now in your goal of breaking the co-sleeping habit as compared to where you were when you responded in Part I of the book to Co-Sleep Quiz 1.

After responding yes or no to each statement in Co-Sleep Quiz 3, look back to you responses to the statements in Co-Sleep Quiz 1. This comparison will help you gauge your progress toward breaking the co-sleeping habit and getting on the path to raising secure children.

Co-Sleep Quiz 3

Put a check mark next to each statement that you agree with.

❏   1.   I want to maintain a strong emotional bond with my children throughout their lives.

❏   2.   I know that I don't have to co-sleep with my child to maintain a strong emotional bond.

❏   3.   I realize that effective parenting, including attachment parenting, means having a plan, not just reacting moment to moment.

❏   4.   I understand that my child will cope better during the day if he or she copes better at bedtime.

❏   5.   I can imagine myself in a leadership role with my children.

❏   6.   I am ready to help my children develop their inner strengths so that they can deal with the changes they will face throughout their lives.

❏   7.   I realize how my own thinking barriers and fears have stopped me from breaking the co-sleeping habit in the past.

❑   8.   I believe my children are ready to learn how to fall
         asleep and stay asleep.

❑   9.   My partner or someone else close to me has agreed to
         support me in the process of breaking the co-sleeping
         habit with my child.

❑   10. I am ready to set the date to break the co-sleeping
         habit with my child.

The following analysis of the statements in Co-Sleep Quiz 3
will help you gauge your progress toward your goals of breaking the co-sleeping habit and raising secure children.

Statement 1

**I want to maintain a strong emotional bond with my
children throughout their lives.**

Checking this statement means that you understand that
bonding, or attachment, does not just apply when your children
are infants and young children. You understand that maintaining
a strong emotional bond with your children is something you
want to and can do throughout their lives.

As your children develop and as their needs change, the
mechanisms for maintaining a strong parent-child bond change
as well. Being a flexible parent who is sensitive and responsive to
your children's changing needs will help maintain the bond both
you and your children want.

Statement 2

**I know that I don't have to co-sleep with my child to
maintain a strong emotional bond.**

If you checked this statement, you understand that you do not have to co-sleep with your children to maintain a strong attachment. If you are following a plan that includes co-sleeping and your children and the rest of the family are responding well to that plan, there is no need to change it. But you don't have to co-sleep to maintain bonding or attachment with your children, even when they are very young.

Strong, loving parent-child relationships are maintained through:

- Open communication
- Showing a true interest in your children's feelings, thoughts, and activities
- Being emotionally available
- Comforting your children with touch and understanding when they feel bad or need encouragement
- Being a good role model who is consistent and reliable and who makes your children feel safe, protected, and valued

Statement 3

I realize that effective parenting, including attachment parenting, means having a plan, not just reacting moment to moment.

If you checked this statement, you have had the important insight that being reactive moment to moment is not effective in meeting your children's needs. If you have been in the co-sleeping habit with your children in reaction to their protests about falling asleep without you or about sleeping through the night independently, you are co-sleeping in a reactive way, not based on a plan or philosophy. Reactive parenting can be exhausting and frustrating as well.

Effective parenting, including attachment parenting, is based on a plan that you think about in advance and then apply with the support of your partner. Your parenting plan, including how to parent at bedtime, should be based on meeting your children's needs and the needs of the family.

Statement 4

I understand that my child will cope better during the day if he or she copes better at bedtime.

If you checked this statement, you are acknowledging the nighttime-daytime connection. You realize that your child's difficulties at bedtime are not isolated but are part of a larger pattern. The way poor coping shows itself varies from child to child, but it can include tantrums, clinginess, fearful behavior, interrupting, or manipulation. You understand that if you can guide your child in coping better with bedtime and sleep, your child will cope better with transitions and challenges during the day. Your child will communicate more appropriately, without whining and manipulation, both at bedtime and during the day.

Statement 5

I can imagine myself in a leadership role with my children.

If you checked this statement, you can imagine yourself in a leadership role with your child. Being able to imagine yourself as a leader, or coleader, in the family is essential for becoming one.

You have learned that being a leader as a parent:

- Is loving—not mean
- Involves being calm and assertive—not screaming or harsh
- Will help make your children feel secure

Children should not be burdened with running the family, even if they seem, at times, as though they want that role. Your taking on the leadership role with your partner will help your children feel safe and protected.

Statement 6

I am ready to help my children develop their inner strengths so that they can deal with the changes they will face throughout their lives.

Checking this statement means that you realize that doing everything for your children is not the answer. Your role as a parent is to help your children develop their inner resources and build on their strengths so that they can deal with the changes they will face throughout their lives. Helping your children develop age-appropriate self-comforting skills and confidence at bedtime so that they don't fear sleeping without you is part of that goal.

Statement 7

I realize how my own thinking barriers and fears have stopped me from breaking the co-sleeping habit in the past.

If you checked this statement, you are on your way to breaking the co-sleeping habit. Being able to recognize and challenge your powerless thinking, your tendency to procrastinate, your blaming others rather than taking responsibility, and your fears of failure will help you follow the steps and guidelines provided in breaking the co-sleeping habit. Recognizing and challenging your thinking barriers and fears will make you a more effective parent and person.

Statement 8

I believe my children are ready to learn how to fall asleep and stay asleep.

If you checked this statement, then you have confidence in your children's ability to learn how to cope with change and separation. You are also acknowledging your own ability to teach them how to fall asleep and stay asleep without your lying next to them. Your confidence in your children will show. They will sense it. This will help them learn the skills they need to fall asleep and stay asleep.

Statement 9

My partner or someone else close to me has agreed to support me in the process of breaking the co-sleeping habit with my child.

If you checked this statement, you have successfully reached out and gained support for breaking the co-sleeping habit. You realize that if your spouse or partner is not in agreement or sabotages the process, things will stay the same. You also realize there may be moments during the process when you will want to give in and that having support will help you follow through with your plan.

Statement 10

I am ready to set the date to break the co-sleeping habit with my child.

Checking this statement means that you are ready to begin. You understand the value of breaking the co-sleeping habit, you have worked through your inner barriers, you have a plan that is appropriate to the age and situation of your child, and you are eager to get started. So go ahead and set the date!

Trust Yourself To Create Positive Change

My goal in writing this book is to encourage you as a parent to be a calm, assertive leader who maintains attachment with your children by being sensitive to their changing needs as they grow. The theme throughout this book has been that raising secure, happy children is an active process that requires you to think about and follow through on plans that you create as you guide your children on their journey toward adulthood.

Raising secure, well-adjusted children requires trusting your own judgment. It requires a willingness and excitement to learn new skills that allow you to grow with your children. It is your trust in yourself as a parent and your confidence in your children's inner resources that will maintain a strong parent-child attachment.

Encourage yourself and trust yourself to create a new parenting plan for bedtime, and follow through. Setting and maintaining better bedtime boundaries requires patience and consistency. It takes time and thought. Take the time that you and your children need to accomplish the milestone of independent sleep.

Making positive changes in how you parent your children can be challenging, but you can do it. It's worth it.

Index

A

ADHD, children with, 165–66
Anger
  dealing with, 36, 94, 112–
    13, 138–39
  in face of change, 36, 85,
    93–94, 138–39
  hate vs., 93
Attachment
  about: overview, 9, 11
  balanced family connections
    and, 23–28, 194–96
  bottom line, 28–29
  co-sleeping compared to,
    12–13
  enmeshment vs., 24–25. *See*
    also Enmeshment
  family bed and, 14–19,
    41–42, 190
  infant insecurity and, 13
  maintaining after infancy,
    20
  overinvolvement and,
    25–28, 71, 81, 127, 148,
    210
  reducing clinginess, 47–48
  self-comfort and, 21–22
  separation anxiety, 21–22,
    43, 98, 118, 173, 175
  shifting gears as child
    develops, 22–23
Attachment parenting, 5,
  12–13, 14, 15, 18–19, 24,
  33, 37, 43–44, 50, 70–71,
  215–16

B

Barriers, internal. *See* Inner
  barriers
Bedtime boundaries. *See also*
  Independent sleep
  by age, overview, 63–64
  limit setting and, 70. *See*
    also Setting limits (with
    toddler and preschooler);
    Breaking co-sleeping habit
    references
  need for, 3, 6
  positive change with, 219

Bedtime boundaries—
continued
  reducing clinginess, 47–48
  tucking in. *See* Tucking in
    and disengaging
Begging, 57–58, 61, 112–13,
  138–39, 176, 183, 209
Blame, 75
  barriers created by, 80–81
  list of people given,
    80–81
  not blaming child for your
    actions, 111, 137
  quiz to identify, 86–95
  stopping and taking control,
    81–83
  stopping and taking control
    of, 217
Breaking co-sleeping habit.
  See also Setting limits (with
    toddler and preschooler)
  about: overview, 63–64
  benefits of, 5
  changing thinking for,
    76–77
  of children and former
    spouse/extended family,
    163–64
  of children co-sleeping
    together, 163
  of children with ADHD,
    165–66
  of ill children, 166–67
  of multiple children,
    161–63
  "parent's manual" tips on,
    5–6

  when going on family trip,
    167
Breaking co-sleeping habit
  (elementary schoolers),
  117–44
  about: overview, 117–18
  adult support for, 123–25,
    137
  anticipating protests, 122–
    23
  avoiding power struggles,
    139
  bedtime routine, 119–22
  checking in with child,
    139–40
  children spending time in
    their room and,
    125–26
  comforting/encouraging
    yourself and, 136–37
  dealing with protests, 138
  encouraging self-comfort,
    133, 134–35
  family meeting for, 125,
    126–29, 163
  following through, 138–39,
    142
  getting child back in bed,
    140–41
  overcoming inner your
    barriers. *See* Inner
    barriers; Leadership
  pre-bedtime prep, 121, 128,
    130–31, 132, 144
  prepping child for, 124–31
  providing comfort/support,
    133–34

reinforcing new habits,
142–44
setting date, 99, 118–19
setting limits, 133
sleeping peacefully after, 142
staying in charge, 132
story of Anthony, Cassie,
and parents, 197–203
story of Audrey and parents,
171–78
story of Benjamin and
parents, 191–96
transition day, 129–31
tuck-in process/
disengagement, 132–36
wind-down time, 119–21,
128, 130, 132, 144, 166
Breaking co-sleeping habit
(preteens and teens), 145–
60
about: overview, 145–46
easy-fix examples, 146–49
Kate's and Jonathan's stories,
149–53
professional help for, 157–60
relaxation techniques for,
153–57
stories of Suzie and Derek,
157–60
story of Charlie and parents,
146–47, 148–49, 205–10
story of Sam and parents,
179–84
story of Tammy and parents,
147–49
when they won't sleep alone,
149–53

Breaking co-sleeping habit
(toddlers and preschoolers).
See Setting limits (with
toddler and preschooler)
Breathing, for relaxation, 154

C
Checking in with child, 112
Confidence
communicating, 68
increased, from independent
sleep, 46–50
Co-sleeping habit
breaking. *See* Setting
limits (with toddler and
preschooler); *Breaking co-
sleeping habit references*
factors defining, 3
ill effects of, 2–3
intentional parenting and,
4, 44, 65–66
reactive approach to, 3–5,
33, 35, 55, 61, 183–84,
188, 194–95, 215–16
responsive parenting and,
3, 4, 12, 20, 24, 33, 43,
214
scenario illustrating, 1–2
Crying, dealing with, 3,
42–43, 56–57, 69, 110–11,
112, 138

D
Disengagement, 109–10,
135–36

Divorced or single parents
   breaking habit if child
      co-sleeps with former
      spouse/family, 163–64
   co-parenting issues, 72
   story of Anthony, Cassie,
      and parents, 197–203
   visitation advice, 164–65

E
Enmeshment, 23, 24–25,
   147–48, 195, 202, 206–7

F
Family bed, 14–19, 41–42,
   190
Family examples
   child starting off/never
      leaving your bed (Lilly/
      family), 185–90
   divorced/single parents
      (Anthony/Cassie/family),
      197–203
   middle-of-the-night wake-
      up (Sam/family),
      179–84
   sneaking into bed
      "unnoticed" (Benjamin/
      family), 191–96
   tucking in (Audrey/family),
      171–78
   ultimate imbalance (Charlie/
      family), 205–10
Family meeting, 125, 126–29,
   163

Fear(s)
   breaking nighttime cycle,
      48–50, 98
   facing challenges and, 45,
      46, 48, 85, 209
   of failure, impeding success,
      83–84, 92–95, 217
   quiz to identify, 86–95

I
Ill children, breaking habit
   with, 166–67
Independent sleep, 41–62
   benefits of, 7, 22–23, 40,
      41–62
   breaking nighttime fear
      cycle, 48–50
   child coping with, 20,
      22–23. *See also* Self-
      comfort(ing)
   Dr. Sears on, 43–44, 85
   Dr. Spock on, 42–43, 85
   increased confidence from,
      46–50
   less clinginess with,
      47–48
   privacy and, 53–54
   reducing manipulation, 45,
      54–58, 123, 216
   reducing sleep interruptions,
      50–53
   transitioning to, 14, 17–19,
      36. *See also* Breaking co-
      sleeping habit
   trying but not succeeding in
      transition to, 35–36

Inner barriers, 73–95
  changing thinking to
    overcome, 76–77
  excuses to procrastinate,
    79–80, 89, 217
  fear of failure, 83–84, 92–95
  powerless thinking, 77–78,
    88, 217
  quiz to identify, 86–95
  self-talk restricting change,
    74–75, 76, 84
Insecurity, 13, 26–28, 36, 84,
  85, 91, 183–84, 202
Intentional parenting, 4, 44,
  65–66

L
Leadership, 65–72
  calm/assertive behavior and,
    69–70
  communicating confidence
    and, 68
  consistency, trust and, 67–68
  for divorced parents, 72
  limit setting and, 70
  partner and co-leadership,
    71–72
  power struggles and, 66–67
  regaining your authority, 71
  trust and, 66–68
Leaving bed, dealing with,
  104, 113–14
Limit setting, 70. *See also*
  Bedtime boundaries; Setting
  limits (with toddler and
  preschooler)

M
Manipulation
  anger, begging and, 112–13,
    138–39
  consistency, trust and,
    67–68
  empowerment without, 55
  giving in to, 33, 43, 57–58,
    189
  reduced power struggles
    and, 56–57, 139
  reducing, with independent
    sleep, 45, 54–58, 123,
    216
Marriage
  family bed and, 16–17
  maintaining, 19–20
Mental imagery, for relaxation,
  156–57
Middle-of-the-night wake-up
  call, 179–84

O
Overinvolvement, 25–28, 71,
  81, 127, 148, 210

P
Powerless thinking, 77–78, 88,
  217
Power struggles
  ADHD and, 164–65
  avoiding, 139, 164–65
  child leaving bed for yours,
    113–14
  confidence and, 68

Power struggles—*continued*
  co-sleeping and, 1–2, 201–2
  getting child back in bed, 140
  leadership and, 66–67
  path of least resistance and,
    187–88
  reducing/eliminating, 56–57
  story of Lilly and parents,
    185–90
  whining, begging and, 58
Pre-bedtime prep, 121, 128,
  130–31, 132, 144
Privacy
  for children, 54, 126
  lacking, 14–15, 16, 24, 52,
    199–200
  for parents, 14–15, 40, 53–54
  right to, 53–54
Procrastination excuses, 79–80,
  89, 217
Progressive relaxation, 155

Q
Quizzes
  to evaluate changes in
    thinking/goals, 211–18
  to identify internal barriers,
    86–95
  for why you are co-sleeping,
    31–40

R
Reactive co-sleeping/parenting,
  3–5, 33, 35, 55, 61, 183–
  84, 188, 194–95, 215–16

Reasons for co-sleeping, quiz
  for, 31–40
Relaxation techniques, 153–57
Responsive parenting, 3, 4, 12,
  20, 24, 33, 43, 214

S
School issues, 172–73, 181, 206
Sears, Dr. William, 12, 20, 24,
  85
Self-comfort(ing), 21–22
  anger and, 112–13, 138–39
  checking in with child on,
    112, 139–40
  disengaging and, 109–10
  encouraging, 21–22, 107–8,
    133, 134–35
  objects, 106
  privacy stemming from, 54
  reinforcing, 143–44, 164
  tasks, 106
  teaching, 60, 84, 91, 105–7,
    139. *See also* Setting
    limits (with toddler and
    preschooler)
  value of, 54, 56, 217
  for yourself, 111, 136–37
Self-talk
  defined, 73–74
  examining, 86–95, 137
  keeping you from changing,
    74–75, 76, 84
  modifying and empowering,
    78, 79–80, 81–82, 85,
    116
  quiz to identify, 86–95

Separation anxiety, 21–22, 43, 98, 118, 173, 175
Setting limits (with toddler and preschooler), 97–116
about: overview, 97–98
adult support for, 101–2
anticipating protests, 101
bedtime routine, 102–5
checking in with child, 112
child leaving bed for yours and, 113–14, 115
comforting and, 107–9
creating positive associations, 100
dealing with begging and anger, 112–13
dealing with crying, 110–11
handling mid-night intrusions, 115
preparing child's space, 99–100
reinforcing and, 116
setting date, 99
sleeping peacefully after, 114
story of Lilly and parents, 185–90
teaching self-control, 105–6
tuck-in process/ disengagement, 108–10
Sneaking into bed "unnoticed," 117, 141, 191–96
Spock, Dr., 42–43, 85

T
This book
as manual for breaking co-sleep habit, 6
overview of, 7
survey done for, 5
Transitions. *See also* Breaking co-sleeping habit
adapting to, 60–61, 62
to bedtime/independent sleep, 1, 14, 18, 38, 40, 45–46, 59–62
fear of, 98
your feelings about bedtime and, 62
Traveling, co-sleeping and, 167
Trust
consistency and, 67–68
in creating positive change, 219
leadership and, 66–68
yourself, 85
Tucking in, that never ends, 171–78
Tucking in and disengaging, 108–10, 132–36, 178

W
Wind-down time, 119–21, 128, 130, 132, 144, 166

About the Author

DR. VALERIE LEVINE grew up in the Bronx in the 1950s and 1960s. At age 16, she graduated as the valedictorian of her high school class and then obtained her B. A., cum laude, from Barnard College where she majored in psychology. In 1975, she earned a Ph.D. in Educational Psychology at the City University of New York where her doctoral studies focused on the processes of learning and cognition in school-age children.

In the late 1970s, she began her career as an associate research psychologist at Educational Testing Service in Princeton, New Jersey where she conducted longitudinal research on parent-child interaction. With funding from the National Institute of Child Health and Human Development, she and her team examined the relationship between mother-child bonding and children's intellectual development. Her desire to become a clinician and work directly with families was rooted in her observations of parents and children through a one-way mirror as a researcher.

Dr. Levine became licensed to practice psychology under the supervision of Dr. Arnold Lazarus, the founder of Multimodal Therapy. To further enhance her insights into children's functioning, she obtained her certification as a school psychologist at Rider University where she was honored with the Graduate Award in School Psychology in 1986. She continued her private practice and also worked as a school psychologist providing counseling and performing psychological assessments in the public schools.

Dr. Levine has been in private practice for more than 25 years working with children, adults, and families. The services she has provided include family therapy, parent education, individual therapy, psychological evaluations, and school consultations. Of all these services, she finds family therapy the most challenging.

Usually, it is the child who is referred for behavior problems, but it is the family that requires treatment. Pediatricians, family doctors, and psychiatrists refer many of the children and families that she treats. Very often, the roles and boundaries in the family are out of alignment the parents feel frustrated and powerless. They often state in the first session that they have tried everything, but this is not the case. She has found that the key to change for many of these families is untangling the imbalances in the parent-child relationship. As a result of applying techniques designed to bring families into balance, the families that she has treated have shown consistent, long lasting gains.

In addition to her private practice, Dr. Levine has given lectures and workshops for parents, teachers, medical doctors, and lawyers on such topics as child abuse, school violence, domestic violence, parenting during divorce, parent-child relationships, positive discipline, and stress management. She was part of a panel who spoke with widows in New Jersey about how to cope with parenting issues after 9/11. During the 1980s and 1990s, she taught psychology courses in developmental psychology and counseling techniques to college and graduate students at Rider University, Fairleigh Dickinson University, The College of New Jersey, and the College of St. Elizabeth.

Dr. Levine is also a published author of articles and books in her field. She has published articles in professional journals in psychology and law on such topics as parent-child bonding, mother-infant interaction, parenting during divorce, and child custody issues. She has published study guides and instructors' manuals to accompany college textbooks in psychology for Harcourt Brace and McGraw-Hill, including an Instructor's Manual for Jerome Kagan's 1981 textbook, *Psychology: An Introduction*. She was a science writer for Johnson & Johnson Baby Products in New Jersey where she published *Minimizing High Risk Parenting*, a book that summarized the proceedings of a Pediatric Round Table. She wrote scripts for videotapes on topics in cognitive therapy for the U. S. Army Chaplain School in Fort Monmouth, New Jersey to train Army chaplains in counseling techniques. It was there that she worked on one such script and taping with Dr. David Burns who had, at that time, recently published *Feeling Good*. After that, she was on the referral list of the University of Pennsylvania Medical Center as a cognitive therapist in New Jersey.

From 2003 through the present, Dr. Levine resides in Hendersonville, North Carolina where she is a licensed psychologist and continues to provide psychological services to individuals and families in her private practice, Better Life Counseling and Wellness. For two years, she facilitated two support groups—one for parents of children with ADHD and another for adults with ADHD. In August 2008, Dr. Levine gave a seminar for parents entitled *The Secrets of Positive Parenting* in which she discussed strategies for meeting the challenges of raising children in our complex society.